GOING IT ALONE

PAUL ZARZYSKI

BP Bangtail Press

Montana
2022

ISBN-13: 978-0-9961560-9-7

Manufactured in the United States of America

Front cover photo: Gordon Stevens
Back cover photo: Jessica Brandi Lifland

Published in the United States by

Bangtail Press
P. O. Box 11262
Bozeman, MT 59719
www.bangtailpress.com

BP

Oh, for just one morning's writing launch,
to become the Poet Crow, the Poet Eagle,
the Poet Hawk or Poet Condor,
soaring, gliding, sharing only the sounds of my words
with the roiling clouds and swirling winds,
with the goddesses of flight, over the Grand Canyon,
sans all concern for literary heights,
not a single page, not one book in my talons
gripping solely the air I need to live on.

For
Elizabeth Ann Dear,
With Love

CONTENTS

The Deep Green Breath I Breathe

Singing Our Most Primal Hymns

Stalking the Euphoric Heart's Thicket

The Body's Most Vocal Gonad

Because I Vow in Blood to Burn

Her Heart-Mind-n-Soul Holy Trinity

Dedications, Acknowledgments, Genuflections...

The Deep Green Breath I Breathe

What's 'it' all about?
'It' is all about everything
being intricately woven
into the tapestry of our natural world,
our Universe—every Poem,
therefore,
an Animistic Psalm.

Dad in the Canopy

Kiss of life, iron-ore-miner-deep,
the root capillaries welcome back
my dad's molecules, his ashes
sifting for the past three years
from the surface where I spilled them,
dashed with a dribble of moonshine,
around each trunk of the fifty-one
thickest maples and oaks. Up into the phloem
goes Leonard, Dad, "hardy lion,"
becoming cambium, branch, lenticels, leaf,
chlorophyll in the crowns—the deep green
breath I breathe, believing
I again inhale my father's first love,
as I did, May 25th, 1951,
looking up in wonder.
                            Arms wrapped
only halfway around the bole
of the ancient, of the holy,
I press my damp cheek into the lost
scripture of bark, into the osmotic
jigsaw puzzle-work, into the reptilian hide
of armored time. What I sense here—
about the strength of flesh, about
the overlapping growth-ringed worlds
of animal with plant, the symbiotic
weave of all that is unknown—
puts religion to rest

in the crypts of its own churches
for good.
          So little stretch left
in my skin turning to parchment
letter-pressed with the bark's star charts,
I bid you to read, in lieu
of this poem, the imprint, the topographic map,
the labyrinth of the mystical
between the lines on the right-hand
page of my face. There, may you learn
the eternal sermon of wind
snapping the top off
the oldest oak in this woodlot—fallen
crown wilting limper by the minute, green
fading to yellow into brown, limbs
like my father's gnarled arms
offering their withered bouquets.
                    No matter
how wrenching the tender metaphor
in every lesson of death
held out to us, we, steadfast, reach back,
our hands clenched to the burled urn
carved from bird's-eye, from heartwood
overflowing with sap, with artesian
blood, with whatever living elixir
spills, in this brief duration of faith,
the dust of the ones we love, away.

Vigil

A voyeur with my face
pressed to the window pane,
yesterday I watched,
marveling the yellow
warbler feasting on green
caterpillar stretched from folded aspen leaf—
my fingertips, pinched
to a pencil's lead end, plucking it
smoothly from cocoon
notebook closed. For supper
last night, I charcoaled
a coil of sausage,
boiled corn on the cob,
tipped a couple
double-hopped lagers,
topped it all off
with a latticed slab
of apple pie. I fed the horses
flakes of their favorite
orchard-grass hay, watched
the Phillies rally
in the eighth, read The Trib,
went to bed, waiting
still at midnight for that one
perfect pitch, that one firm word,

to drive home the defining
stanza's final run. This morning,
up before dawn, I have my prostate
to thank, or blame, for this
poem you are reading
or hearing me read aloud. Now,
if we could only savor it,
somehow make it last
longer—the whole
squirming segmented length,
all 39 lines of its being
becoming flight, emerging
as bird, winged and singing
into thin, unforgettable air.

Blood and Ink

I am the father of this page. It
inherits its twisted DNA
helix spliced with genes, its Y
chromosome, from its sire, me. I give
it life by infusing these lines
with their four humors, by filling the long dry
cylindrical bones with marrow, each
capillary with unique corpuscular bump
and roll, the heart with meaning far
beyond its rhythmic beat. I dub its soul
otherworldly—grace
it with an uncanny knack to shift
shape, change color, mutate
molecular make-up.
                        When gas,
the soul can be one *hell*
of a stitch. On the liquid flip side,
what a sometimes viscid,
sometimes slick and unwieldy,
demanding bastard. The soul,
thank goodness, seldom turns solid
because no weak-kneed bipod, no
gravity-curbed biped earthling, ever
could bear its meteorite heft. I have
zero control over the soul

after I have fashioned its jacket
of latticework.
                    Yes, I am the father,
but merely the mortal father, of this poem
fancied, forged, born, begot
on Father's Day. For years to come,
we will offer the stars homage
for this one-of-a-kind episode
defining us both for life. The poem and I
will meet, third Sunday in June,
on some familiar, deserted wilderness trail
long ago brushed-over. We,
happily lost, will embrace,
exchange cards, read one another's
greeting aloud, then go on going
our separate ways until we find where
the other has already left
kindred imprints in the wild grass. You see,
history mimics its simple self,
and what is history if not
lives relived, places revisited,
moments cloned—the constant chopping
chopping echo of progeny off the old block.

Aphorisms, Adages, Maxims, and Pavlov's Silvertip

Ashes to ashes, dust to dust. Here today,
gone tomorrow. What goes around
comes around. An eye for an eye,
a tooth for a tooth, and man is not the one
and only large carnivore
who cannot live on bread alone,
whose home is where the heart is,
in Montana, where grizzlies have learned to
(because you can't teach an old dog
new tricks, but that saw doesn't hold
sway for an old sow) come a-running
toward rifle-shot dinner bell
gut piles during elk season
when the early bear, as the saying goes,
always get the liver.
                        In Montana, big
bad wild canines, and felines, also know
urban sprawl happy hour
precedes "supper is served"
at the all-you-can-eat Ranchette Estates
Buffet, where it's okay to bite
the hand that feeds you—

front porch hors d'oeuvres,
Science Diet appetizers,
garbage can canapés, dumpster
munchies, ThunderShirted
lapdogs and Reebok'd joggers
à la carte. Sometimes a carnivore's
eyes are way, *way* bigger
than its stomach. Sometimes you
eats the b'ar, sometimes
the b'ar eats you. Because beauty,
you see, truly *is* in the eye of the beholder
beholding the watched
pot boiling over and over.

Click...Click...

Predator eye honed,
since turning BB-gun-five,
to its feathered edge, I catch
the ruffed grouse flashing
its neon-red failure
to blend into the November gray-
black bed of quaking aspen leaves
matching the bird's mottled jacket
not quite exactly. It cocks
its head, eyes me up
and down, crouches,
stretches, sets
sleek-plumed for the raucous
launch that trips my neurons
to cue my arms vaulting into the shotgun's
buoyant choreography, into the *port de bras*
wings of the poised
ballerina on point.
                              I **click**
the safety off. With this brisk slap
smack across the ear of silence, I take bead
while silence, in defiance, turns
its tearful cheek. The bird fading
out of range—fifty years of habit sapped

just like that—I *click*
the safety back on. What unfamiliar
whisper from behind the scrim
is this that flips the trigger
finger's dimmer switch,
helix-deep, to soothe us
into beatific bloom? Thrilled,
bedazzled by the shattered jagged bits
of fragile masculinity, I jig
and juke down rocky slope, shotgun
shells jumping in my jacket
pockets like maracas keeping tempo
to a syncopated pulse.
                              Grappling
the sinewy old pickup truck's steering
wheel over badger-holed meadow
back to gravel road—my Montana
manhood dancing in the cab with mistresses
I no longer need to please by squeezing
off the shot—we rock
into a requiem dusk, our roughed-up hearts
drumming hot, our knuckles, white
with love, bloodied only on the inside.

Humanely Askew

Long before I squeezed the trigger for real,
became predator and believed it
a rite of adolescent passage
to hit the bars, pursue trophy women,
toss back shots and beers,
long before Saturday night
mimicked the opening morning of big game
hunting season—rural towns
surrounded by the wooded
homes of our animal brethren
over whom, the Bible rules, man shall lord
his dominion—long before I turned
manly in Antlered-Tavern, America,
I slept with stuffed animals,
my favorite bear doll
decked out in his Montana Peak ranger hat,
suspendered denims, and belt buckle embossed
with his name, Smokey.
                                        Forty-five years later,
long after confessing my predatory sins,
from "fair chase" to Saturday night
rituals in wild saloons, after biting hard my lip
to keep from weeping a child's tears
beside the grave of the real Smokey
the Bear in Capitan, New Mexico,
another cub, Burnie, survives

the Bitterroot Forest Fires, summer of 2000,
stirring up in us the anthropomorphic embers
never lying dormant for long, warming
what little is left of the soul
just beneath the smoldering soil.
                              "Delivered from evil,"
his paws scorched, Burnie graces us
with yet one more chance to showcase
our newsworthy pathos, our knack
for doing some godly good. We swaddle his paws,
nurse Burnie's wounds through months
of painful oozing, applaud his first tender steps
into a soothing coolness. We lay him down
to sleep with fellow bruin
snoozers. Come April, we celebrate his waking
reunion with the wilds, his playful
traipsing cued by so little instinct
through summer into the fall,
into the open, open season, open rifle sights
framing all eighty pounds
of his salvaged life into maybe one
grocery bag of "harvested" meat
and bear cub rug—lustrous
teeth reflecting the ferocious
hopelessness preying on us all.

Matinee Western

Thrilled by the cinnamon bruin rolling on ball-
bearing shoulders and hips
through tall green needlegrass—the sumo
floating into his choreographed
dance with flora's sinewy
ballet troupe on this shimmering
Montana hillside stage
to a sold-out house of "nature's people"
awestruck behind the scrim—how
can we *not* choose to believe
this kinetic bear, sans gravity,
solos, spot-lit, solely for we two
winners of tickets to the premiere
we're viewing from our pickup truck cab
orchestra pit seats we gaze up from
mesmerized by this wild-
west live performance
we applaud with our most pious silence.

Starling Seeing Stars

Living inside of a bass drum
what a thunderous echo
when its kick-pedal mallet thump
plasters wet feathers
to the picture window—the unloved,
un-colorful, un-humming bird, breast-up,
dead, is my best un-veterinarian guess.
                              But why
not feel deserving of just one up-tempo note
of miracle, of beauty, of musical
score to adorn the usual morning
dirge of world news
saturated with tragedy, rage,
hatred, anguish, fear?
                    What else is there
if not the infinitesimal long shot
bet against heaven's deaf ear, bet
in favor of one bird's rung bell fading
back into silence, into the primal grace
of flight making my day?
                        From writing
desk to window to coffee pot back to desk,
thirty-odd anxious round trips

later, I find the bird upright,
squatting all a-wobble at first
before perching, wood-carving-stiff,
on its stick pins, its head tucked
into a wing as lovely as a trumpeter swan
a-slumber on calm water.
                          In the wake
of this still-life pose held forever, this *un*living
proof of vertical rigor mortis, I sign
the death certificate, write the eulogy,
carve the tombstone, dress in undertaker black,
fetch the garden spade from the tool shed
and ...*wait*! What's *this*? Well I'll be
an ugly duckling's uncle. Look.
Look!
          Is it really preening its feathers,
stretching its wings like people do their arms
after a power nap, the comic-strip thought
bubble above its thunked
noggin reading, "Where in the flock
did everybody go?"
                          "Into thin air, *Dude*!"
I thought-bubble my response, my forehead
plopped against the feathered pane

the instant the bird blasts off.
                              I praise angels,
blather hosannas to the ornithological gods,
pour my lucky-charmed heart into a litany
of contrition—"I *do* renounce Avian
Satan, I *do* renounce Avian Satan"—
as I pray my way to the kitchen sink
where I *do,* I *do,* I *do* renounce
Avian Satan, that sky-blue serpent,
Windex, coiling down the drain.

Woodnotes to the Churchgoing Woodcutter

Not that I want to be a god or a hero. Just to
change into a tree, grow for ages, not hurt anyone.
Czeslaw Milosz

You claim to trust in God, His law
to love thy neighbor as thyself? Then you must
believe this century-old cottonwood
tree, standing monumentally before you and far beyond
its fecund budding years, is still God's
darling, holding, in its gnarled arms,
in its clenched fists, more of God's infinite sky
than it ever held when hefting
the heavy fleece of leaves from which it took
seven wintry months to catch
its breath. You claim to believe
death is, in fact, the vital first step
toward eternal afterlife you know exists
but cannot picture? Simply look up.
Flip your chainsaw's toggle switch
to OFF. Step closer. Press your pious ear
into the lichened bark. Sigh deep to the heart-
wood singing "home sweet home"
to fliers and climbers looking on
through all of time, not one whit—no matter
what piffle the Bible posits—the lesser
of God's harmonious notes. Stop. You better
step far back. Peer hard and long

through the nearby cabin's windows. See yourself,
pen in hand, sitting at the marble altar
inside—pondering the maestro
you claim to believe in, Him
tirelessly conducting with infinite wands
His symphonies. Listen to the music of the universe
unfurled by earth's oldest virtuosos
creating more warmth than the firewood
of this one tree you could choose not to cut—
choose, soulfully, not to forever burn.

Tripping Timber

The haunted sawyer squints down his swath,
eyes bloodshot from the flog of sawdust,
exhaust, sun flaring
off pools of stump pitch.
                                    Bees.
Bloodhound bees. All morning,
dazzled by the chainsaw's blur
and skirl—indiscriminate
frenzy of teeth and rakers
into flesh—these bees go crazy
for resin.
              His mind runs
rich to the hinge-wood dirge,
to that full-throttled lull—timber
tripped off its stump,
limbs unfolding like wings
in a long stroke of lift
before the plummet.
                              He relives the green
kid opening a leg to the bone
while tripping a hollow larch, crural
arteries like blown hydraulics
pumping him empty, the heart
pounding against strong torque

his partner put to the tourniquet,
and worker bees swarming
that warm red nectar.
                                  Sun cauterizes
the fresh stump he drowses against
during lunch—heartwood
bound in concentric rings, the vortex
into his worst recurring dream
where forest he's cut becomes a ward
of amputees.
                        Hordes of phantom bees
rouse him out of the tormenting
shards and sparks
spray of saw chain
biting into the hot, blue heart of the hive.

Missoula Eulogy, Lunar Perigee, Great Falls Revelation

"Where the Christ is Jesus when He's needed
most?" I wish I'd have had the *huevos*
profane enough to pray like an anarchist
archangel with arms
cross-boned over my ruffled brisket,
over my scarred heart thumping from the pulpit
of my first, and goddamned last, First Presbyterian
Church packed to the rafters with sadness
exacting its tangible red
lava lamp of viscous roil—slow-
motion amoeboid agony writhing just as I,
terrified by grade school catechism,
once imagined souls suffering in molten hell
behind fireproof glass.
                              I acquiesced. I did
as I was asked. I piously recited to the mournful
my poetry from The *Pretty Good* Book
According To Zarzyski—chapter nonexistent,
page-you-name-it, verse whatever-
the-infidel-hell. After the last shot-glass toast,
I drove pie-eyed into the high-beam
moon looming closer—God
on a Harley hog—closer. Tipping
both visors down to cut the glare
off black ice, I fought

the Monte Carlo's steering
wheel pulling hard
left as if beckoned by the light
of the oncoming.
           Thanks, but no thanks,
to my gymnastic grip and crapulent
migraine that kept me thinking *right, right,*
right up to the penitential moment I revved
into the garage and out of the Stones' crescendo'd
"Sympathy for the Devil," I made it safely home-
sweet-home.
           Pressing the Chevy's heavy hood above my head,
I wept, at long last, for my dead friend, as I glimpsed the radiant
halo lathed deep into the sagged steering shaft
rubbing against the frame with each dip,
swale, swerve of my s-curved life—the thrice-blessed
dumb luck of a bucking-horse-rider, minus
that one wrong bronc, of a timber-faller,
minus that one rotted snag, of a brash
sad traveler, minus that one sharp
turn-too-many into the Godly dark.

Informally in Memoriam

Cocktail-hour autumn sun accents every cat-
scratched inch of short stroke, each
centimeter-deep groove
raked into Ranch Oak
kitchen table leg—a block
of Asiago or stick of frozen butter
a Windows on the World gourmet chef
scored with fork tines
over a florid seafood dish
lightly garnished.
               Blonde wood shards on the dark
short-napped carpet—suddenly shagged
around this one leg mornings ago—
collared our torrid nocturnal waltzer
curled in her cardboard box
by the wall heater and meowing
for her geriatric chow—the old
log house creaking as it warmed,
rousing from a night of reminiscent bear
claws honed cambium-deep
into living trees.
               Decades after
our cat, Georgia, died, we peeled
the clear wide vertical strips of tape
from her favorite table leg, refinished the rest,

left her legacy as a light-
hearted epitaph to a simpler place
in time. Today, September 11, 2001,
I try to multiply that sadness of one
sudden absence of tiny life
by an Arabic number far too large,
far too unreal, for naming. I am feebly able
to offer my grief for what little I know
I can stomach, know I can grasp,
here and now—sipping a stiff drink,
biting my nails to the painful quick.

Last Stand—May 25, 1951, to...

My place of final unrest has chosen me,
should our Mother Ship go up in smoke,
down in flames, sideways through Her
berserk lost-hubcap spin-off into the black
orbital dead-end dark with yours truly,
my ticket punched, still on board
for the short ride. I vow to hold on
tight beneath this windy green
photosynthetic canopy of "The Twenty"
acres of exalted hardwoods
my father willed me to foster
via his very DNA, his everlasting
blue-collar genome, resurrected
from root hairs into the radiant
welcoming wings of the 51
maple, ash, oak, birch
I spread his remains beneath
like stardust. I will throw
my arms around the sturdiest
trunk with the humbling courage
Dad summoned from the earth
bidding him adieu. He did not pray
to be spared, but to be taken
with grace, as I, yearning the same,
will face the sentimental
song's closing riffs of acorns

clacking their typewriter staccatos
off the steel roof of the shack
Dad dubbed in hand-carved letters
arched above the door,
S E R E N I T Y. Here, I will receive
my last rites sacrament
of respiration, the sacred
exchange of water for wine within
the tabernacle's pink
satin tissue of the lungs. With this
parting molecular gift
exhaled into me
through pores of my father's trees
granting what crippled miracles, what
wounded mercies, they still can grant
from earth's deathbed, I will beg
their forgiveness with my final breath.

Singing Our Most Primal Hymns

Will somebody please tell the guy
in the wheelhouse of the Large Hadron Collider
that we Poets have long-ago defined the 'God Particle'
as a single raindrop, a single snowflake, one teardrop
shed in the name of love and loss.

Salt Water Love

I. Wishing

If these inland waves were home to belugas,
white whales bugling
their pod ensembles, their brass-
wind movements through cherry orchards
in blossom—if gold dust floated,
if this pollen we glide through were gold,
this canoe, white birch, then
wouldn't whales take us for one of their own
flecked rich? Wouldn't love
lob-tailing over this water
become a visible breeze, a spoondrift medley
of fragrance and taste, an epicure's
blend of semi-sweet? Wouldn't love be made
so tangible we could handle it,
the way osprey mates hold
an immense ponderosa snag
balanced in their talons, keeping it
tall with dignity long beyond its green life?

II. Beachcombing With Sharron

To write a love poem worthy of the sea,
become a sailor, or meet Her your first time
in the dark-eyed soundings of a goddess so lovely
she knows the cosmos is the ocean's clone,
she hears the whale concerto capsuled

orbital through outer space. I am 26,
single, a fresh-water Midwesterner
come to Half Moon Bay to learn to love
a bigger part of earth—Pacific,
my first mistress, first spindrift
rigadoon with surf, tide pool roundelay
with two beauties. I come to love
the whale's eye, small as an orange,
big as a human heart, to love
the sea anemone, the reason
all souls turn inward when touched.

III. Sea Legs

Never in cowboy boots
having toted a woman
piggyback over tide pools—
midwinter rock, slick with kelp
and ice glaze—I am certain
today is a day to love sailors. All
because you believe in this wild horse
like a seaworthy ship beneath you,
believe the yarns I've spun of a boy
raised on risk in the arctic Midwest,
how he'd gallop slick-shod
over the streetlight glare

off black ice, seldom lose all ballast
and when he did, could right himself,
his arms like flippers or fins
gripping an equilibrium
within the riptide. The Atlantic applauds
the sturdy pitch and roll of you
aboard my vertebrae—the true love
real sailors feel
only when living on thrill.

IV. How the Beluga Spoons

For a whispered secret or to steal a kiss, I lean out
over her tank, like a ship's figurehead,
far as a man in love dare reach
without altogether letting go. My fingers grip the rail
behind me, arms contorted to flippers. Rippling
in this aquamarine mirror, a human face
becomes the face of a whale
nosing cautiously through
the surface, that crystalline plane
between two worlds. I smile, her lips opening
into her eye-to-eye cavern. I throw a kiss, toss it
gently with a nod. She dips her lower jaw,
scoops it full as a waterwheel bucket,
and with a gesture, rightly larger,
wetter, more deliberate than mine,

approves our courtship. She chortles
my comic response, my straight-man nonchalance,
ladles another mandible full, and showers me
again with kisses. By this passage, we vow
to the cosmos a romance revived
from eons of dormancy. We feel our way,
sonar and sight, slowly
into the gray swales—lovers
sounding our one laughter
wave after wave, quasar to quasar,
toward that first rollicking spark and whatever
leviathan god brought it on.

Heart

Forked to the jump-n-kick brushstroke,
forelock to fetlock, into the vast
landscape of canvas, into the open
range of paper, otherwise known as "time
and space," it takes the painter
who has perched the hurricane
deck of the Equus tempest
to sense how everything equine
begins and ends wildest
at the withers.
         Above the horse's heart
press your coarse ear to the soft
nimbus of bristle. Listen, breath
stilled, to this stirring of rides lived,
lived into the oils, into the sumi ink,
watercolor, charcoal, crayon, into the medium
of sheer air—oh, sweet molecule, sweet melody—
into the prehistoric flesh-n-blood
contortioned defiance of horse
anatomy, all static wooden-model study
bushwhacked at the academic pass.
                With back hooves
splitting the nuclei of Nevada high desert
air into thin infinities of contour line,
don't we stake our claim to all

big bang fallouts—of creation, of desolation—
the imagination's afterglow, like the bronc
hip-cocked, at rest, for our graced glimpse
into the mystery?
                    Let us now sing
our most primal hymns from the cave
walls of Chauvet, of Lascaux,
to gallery walls everywhere still echoing
the heavy-gaited riddle echoed deep from within
all time and space: what *is* the soul
if not the heart in flight, both aura and form,
soaring before us toward the light,
the light its ancient self
illuminated by this one, blazing
musical movement of truth, the horse.

Pilgrimage—Great Falls, Montana, 1995

I still love the West...as I love an old horse, for what she was.
Charlie "Kid" Russell

From my porch across 4th Avenue North,
you too would marvel at the processions—
stalwart-hearted cowboys
(you can peg them by their gait)
on worshipful journeys to
Charles M. Russell's log cabin
studio. Even at this distance,
I see them itching to quit the trail-
broke bunches of tourists—see them
straining to "cheek" the unruly-colt instinct
to step out where Kid Russell stepped
from terra firma into the stirrup of his Meanea
Saddle cinched to Monte, Red Bird,
Neenah, their shod hoofprints
stamped, tooled, burned deep into the leather
core of this hallowed ground
long before the grooming
of bunchgrass prairie into manicured lawn
currycombed and roached.
                              In their highfalutin,
fuming "skunk wagon" diesel
breeds of all stripes, they ride in
a century and a quarter after their forefathers,
one-hundred and twenty-five times

wilder, rode in drunk
on the bronc-buster musk of saddle blankets
lathered.
          Their cattywampus parallel parking
speaks comical volumes. I, sipping
my fifth whiskey ditch, mumble to myself
"He's not here now, boys! Come again
after the first Alberta Clipper rolls
the calendar pages of this neighborhood
back eighty years!"
             To those most reverent few
removing their beaver lids as they break
the plane into the sanctum, I want to whisper how,
late one Christmas Eve, *I swear*, I saw
firelight behind his crimson curtains, smoke
cut, without a trace, clean away
at the chimney's lip by a palette knife wind
swirling, sculpting snow
drifts into apparitions that left me
chilled beside my own hearth
glowing hot. To Charlie's buffalo skull
insignia looming through the storm
like a crucifix in cowpuncher church, maybe
I should have sung "Silent Night," prayed

Badger Clark's "A Cowboy's Prayer." Instead,
Kid's rounder rendition of "The Night
Before Christmas" was the verse I caroled,
my breath melting a porthole into a glazed pane
as I belted out with simple glee
and glory be:
> "I've knowed of men a-havin' snakes
> And others swarms of bats.
> Some had spiders in their clothes
> And turkeys with plug hats.
>
> Ol' whiskey was to blame for this
> For drinkin' was the cause.
> I guess I'll have to quit the booze
> Cuz I got Santy Claus."

                                              And thus, they too—
these time-traveled venerators of the Old West—
appear out of a blizzard of tradition, of myth,
out of a boozy Blue Norther lineage,
legacy, birthright or legend
beckoning them
to track whatever sign, to heed whatever song line,
lodestar, lead steer, guides them across
frontiers, across generations, the Great Divide,
spiritual time, across this narrow city street
into the everlasting past of heroes

distilled on canvas, leavened into clay,
still gracing us with belief
in our most sobering faiths—Charlie Russell,
the holiest cowboy ghost I have ever known.

Prophecy

He always stirs before the graphic
end of life on earth begins
its final countdown, the winged
cylinder's accelerated fall
blurring its hieroglyphic-
Sanskrit-graffiti-like universal
truth we will all, in unison, come to
understand, he says, the instant before
it hits. His bedside
notebook lit, aurora borealis
pouring through the skylight,
he sketches this recurring dream scenario,
the vessel's shape and symbols, with each
air-raid alarm sirening him
out of sleep. He believes in and trusts
his simple, clear language
describing the essence of pure peace
coupled with love, the elliptical
identical puzzle parts
by the tens of thousands
somehow fitting, somehow
connecting perfectly together in what he learns
about eternity. He tells me
he is always in physical touch
with his horses, his dogs. Animals
become the angels who return

his veterinary favors and feats,
who save *him*—he knows this for sure
though he's not yet dreamt
near enough the fail-safe point
to sense precisely how. He reaches down
beside the bed, feels the thick fur
of his Red Heeler, eases the other
hand upon his wife
restless beside him. Night, sky, dog,
horse, man, woman, earth, is all
the animal faith, all the heaven, he,
falling back to sleep, will ever need.

Somnambulism

It is inevitable, trust me, that you will rise
but not shine one morning—most likely
after your mother's death—without a friend
on earth and feeling as if you've exited
the womb for a second time,
as if everything in your newborn world
is, well, just like you, new. There's a good chance
you'll need to believe, in the midst of this
cosmic awakening, that you, too, have died
and gone to heaven. Or, more real, more apt,
since death's happy heavenly ending
could be all a ruse, a human-spun
fairy tale, you'll believe instead
simply that you've fallen,
taken an Ambien-induced doozy
of a sleepwalking digger, rung your bell
on the porcelain commode or the linoleum
kitchen floor or the plate glass patio door—
this far-fetched black-out scenario
complicating ten-fold the riddle
you've awoken to?
                    Okay. So this is what
you think you know, but maybe did not want to
know for certain: 1) Old Saint Pedro
has not punched your salvation ticket

at the Pearly Gates. Nor has Satan
hot-shotted you through the red-hot
one-way turnstile into Hades (likely
more akin to Antarctica, actually, than
to Vegas). And 2) You have not become
an amnesiac after a bad fall. "What's left
then?" you ask aloud to no one in earshot,
not even yourself. I'll tell you "what's left." You are
alive. Let's state that for the record. You
are alive and alone in some brave new world
on the morning after departing
some petrified old world. What more
can you expect after your first breath
than your next breath? Go ahead,
inhale, take it in. Now
another. And another, and...*there*—
your re-entry is complete. Just...keep...breathing...

Why Northerners Pray More

Because they know the soul is not
nocturnal. On the contrary,
it is afraid of the dark, cowers
at the cold, hates that whiskered devil,
winter solstice, loves summer,
celebrates the vernal
equinox as if it were its own
offspring. The soul equates
darkness with sleep and, therefore,
though it may be friend to the body,
sleep is foe to the soul. On moonless nights
it curls up like a cat
hoping to stay sinfully warm,
vigilantly alert around the sacred
little purgatorial light
folks up north are sure to keep lit
down their long, eternal, windowless halls.

Enlightenment

On what would have been Dad's ninetieth
birthday, I forget to blow out the candle
lit in his loving memory, and so
it flickers in the living
room all night long where I,
too, spar with the dark, where
I toss but do not dare turn
on the couch, my arm in a rigid sling
after shoulder surgery. Wincing
in sync with the tiny light that will not die out, I
know why my life tonight wants not
one goddamned thing
to do with metaphor
or myth, with religion or the nouveau-
chic, all-too-quotable, antediluvian
teachings of the Sufi poet, Rumi.

Darkroom Fixer

Three young men pose in a morning-after
snapshot on a Sacramento side street
the man in the middle lives on—the other
two, bookending him in cowboy hats,
passing through for a night on the town
before hauling home to Montana
the hot-off-the-assembly-line bronze
Miley Custom 2-horse trailer
back-dropping the three, all grinning
in defiance through their hangovers, all
effervescent with friendship, all gloating
through the cool hubris of youth.
                                    Scroll down
fifty years. Only one of the friends still
drinks to this Kodachrome ghost
photo fading before him, the trio
dimmed deeper into the bronze finish
with each sip from his last half-
glassfuls of rationed breaths—all three men
oxidizing with the trailer's paint
beneath the print's fixer, beneath
the print's gloss. He ponders whether

to scribe names, place, date onto the shot
as provenance, but opts not to.
                              Instead,
oh how it tickles him to leave it
all to the fancy of some picker, maybe
rummaging some same Sacramento thrift store
the man in the middle shopped often
for old-west memorabilia, "cowboyana,"
vintage kitsch. Drawn deeper into this reverie,
he pictures the whimsical collector
exclaiming in his faux-western drawl
to the woman ringing up the six-bit sale,
"They sure don't build 'em like *that*
anymore, now do they, ma'am?"

Gumbo

It drives me mad, it breaks my heart,
to think of it as the pancreatic
cancer of Montana road that takes me
back to pavement from the dark
bedroom of a cowboy friend
trying not to die
anywhere but here on the foothills ranch
he lives for. To hell
with poetic simile, with histrionics
and histology of mud, of words
every bit as impotent
as the pressure washer's spray,
like medicine, like penance,
never quite reaching deep enough
up into the underworld's unknown
to chip what's evil
completely away—the drip-drip-
chemo-drip of long shot odds.
                              I cling to
nothing now but loss—my head caked
dense with residues of heyday
rodeo escapades long gone—
and loss, at times like these, draws the flow
of logic into sunken clods. Holding
vigil from a spindled chair, I,
the closest to a crucifix
in this room, slump, chin to chest,
forearms to thighs, black
hat in hands between my knees

near the bed where he ropes horns
of *Corriente* steers in morphine dreams. I think
twice of throwing open the drapes
to wake him to October's first wet snow
that he might only see as his last
first wet snow. "Just add water,"
reads the label on my gray matter
box of hardened thought. "Time for me
to hit the gumbo trail," I quip—
his good-bye grin shrinking
so quickly back to grimace.
                           Swallowed
to the hubs in ruts that thrust us out
slicker than they suck us in—chaws of mud
spit up over the hood, the windshield
thickened to adobe wall—my Ford
half-ton skids carnival-ride sideways
between borrow pits, as I,
fighting to stay afloat, lean,
Carhartt-pocket-deep,
out the window farther than I have ever before
leaned to see where I'll someday hope
to steer. Just as long as not
one more saline drip of grief,
("god*damn* you, Paul")
soaks the sunken cheekbones of this
saturated road, then, and only then,
maybe we'll make it, we'll make it—maybe
we'll *both* get lucky enough to make it.

For Judy, Simply "Judy"

Under the influence of six decades of dread
late some night, say we click
open an email labeled "Judy,"
simply "Judy." Say we then find ourselves
strapped into the capsule or wheelhouse—
to the captain's bridge of this poetry
ship on its cryptic mission. Gawking,
say we find our catatonic selves
loathing the control
panel with its lone rotund wall clock—
no gauges, radar, compass, nothing but
this Catholic classroom eye of Cyclops
God, its everlasting second hand
marching in place, marching not
one stiff notch forward, not one
circumference increment
per tick of locked-up torment.
                              The time clock
tolls no knell, no cuckoo, no chime
for Judy, simply "Judy," choosing not
to stay one non-second longer in this
inflamed waiting room of stasis, in this
crazed maze-work of pain, in this
pillory, this purgatory, this earth's
eternal chamber of torturers
smirking their wicked smirks, grinding
their high-voltage heels into her

purple fingertips slipping, one-by-merciful-one,
back into the pink. The winged heart
bled dry, in sync with the will
winded of its give-a-shit,
makes not one guttural utterance of regret
fluttering toward the un-haloed glint
of songs unsung.

> Thus, let us now *not*

fucking pray. Nor turn to some limp page
in our mimeographed hymnals. Let us listen
instead to the breathlessness of the one
mountain stream un-fished, the one sentence
pounding to an emailed pulp
news of one more soul gone AWOL. Let us
trust in the bejeweled
brutality of this roll-call silence—just
as a child, genuflecting
among cassocks, chalices, stained glass, *must*
believe in the presence of the absentee. Straight-
jacketed in our captain's chairs
of catechism, let us choose maybe to glimpse
her riff of molecules, her musical notes—Judy,
simply "Judy"—drifting into the beatific
infinity of song too holy to hear? Ah, hell,
it's all just the same black-holed faith—stars dying,
starving for light—in a time with a mind all its own.

Life after Death

We should seek the greatest value of our action.
Stephen Hawking

The morning after catching wind of one
more friend's death, I move with two
times the lilt in my step, inhale
so deeply into my life-buoy lungs and hold
for so long that my cells scream in unison,
"Let it go! Set it free! Let it all
out!" One carbon dioxide molecule at a time
through the turnstile, I heed the godly
advice, while already scheming the next
body full, mind full, psyche full,
until each conscious act of deep
breathing becomes the awarding of
another grand prize—Pulitzer, Grammy, Oscar,
slot machine jackpot spilling forth,
Hail Mary pass spiraling, slow-motion,
down into my magnetic hands. To the victory
thrill of everything magical,
immaculate, mystical, mysterious—
to that little pair of autonomic feats,
heartbeat and breath—I vow
never again to take for granted
the one-hundred-thousand-plus
"lub-dub lub-dubs," the twenty thousand-

plus "in-with-the-good, out-with-the-bad"
daily exchanges in the Fort Knox vault,
in the tabernacle chalice, in the Wild
West strongbox we can bank on
for the next long-shot second, *if*
we're on the receiving end
of luck's graceful roll of the genome dice—*if*...
if...and only *if*...and even then, just maybe?

Arterial Hemoglobin Blood-Oath Resolution

We are stardust brought to life, then empowered
by the universe to figure itself out—
and we have only just begun.
                    Neil deGrasse Tyson

Long past high noon, it's high time I begin
dialing down the volume
on life's noise—threadbare friendships,
soap-opera psychodramas of the ultra-needy,
all egos, foremost my own, obsolete
deities, icons, heroes, gurus,
long-dead etiquettes, rituals, legacies,
feigned acquaintanceships with faith,
fortune, fame, good and evil,
right and wrong, every frigging single
nuance of myth and melodrama,
from pipe dream to nightmare. In this
absence, this absolute void
filled with horizon-less grace, only
then will The Holy Quartet—Time,
Space, Heartbeat, Breath—beam
radiantly down upon me
that one pure truth that fuels us
to create, to create, to create
solely for the sake of reflecting back

out into the deepest reaches,
into the sparkling particles
colliding by the billions
at the speed of silence, the very
silence out of which we
first shined, into which I now
vow, thanks to Infinity's giving-ness,
to shine again, to begin again, and *again*.

Double Sixes, Double Six-Guns

How silly to kick this histrionic
countdown off again now, coming sixty-six,
after punching the stopwatch
fifty-five years ago, while tracking
with futility, the second-
hand seconds of Alcatraz-
colossal, Arabic-numeral'd,
Catholic grade school wall clocks
defining stasis, stock-still, not so much
keeping breathless time hobbled,
tethered, on a tight leash,
as keeping it caged in an 8-by-8 cell,
the *tick-tick, tick-tick*
torturous march to nowhere,
the pacing in place, the evil tease
keeping us forever just shy
of legal driving age, of legal passion-
pit drinking-n-screwing age—that *tick-tick*
satanic plot of nuns
withholding our Holy Grail, depriving us
of our God-given youth.
            Little could I have
known back in those Vatican-victim sixties
how a lifetime of clocks accelerate into one
animated blur of optical illusion. How,
someday, coming to loathe time-
lapse photography, I would instead

opt for cinematic slo-mo—*The Long Riders*
soaring in a buckjump *grand jeté*,
crashing through old-west-
store-front window panes, shattered
glass, sans gravity, twirling,
twirling into the personal eternity
I now, finally, know and love
as purgatorial bliss. And how I would opt
instead for a Sam Peckinpah Gatling gun
massacre, *The Wild Bunch* paladins
galloping in, nonchalant,
their saddlebags packed with sticks
of dynamite, with life's lit-fuse minutes
greeting destiny and cheating death
in the very same breath, as it *should* be—each
notch, each scene, carved into the beating
red-rock storyboard of the heart
pounding down to one more sunset
we might live just long enough
to ride slowly off into, if
we, the quick, can out-shoot the clock.

Stalking the Euphoric Heart's Thicket

*Never let the page show your age—**Never!***

Time, and Time Again

Time is a pair of yellowed bone-dice in a rawhide cup.
                    Red Shuttleworth—*Hardly Alone*

A good 2:29 a.m. to you, ma'am. And how apt
not to fritter away even more time
standing in the Time Refund line. You're the best-
kept secret in this dimension and...well...
you bet, I *would* like to return in full
all of my wasted time to date. It's all here,
chronicled in these two handfuls of five-
terabyte thumb drives, right
down to the squandered second,
minute, hour, day, week, month, and, yes,
doggone it, year—may the stopwatch gods
please forgive my pissing away
in the sixties one of the latter?
                              What's that
you say? *Very* funny, ma'am. I guess
I do, in fact, seem to have quite a bit of time here
in my hands? So, then—what will it take
to re-credit my account? And, while you're at it,
to rewind, as well, the old
Zarzyski physiological clock, in turn
un-wrinkling these wrinkles, un-graying
this gray you see—the bald spot
and swollen prostate you don't?
                              Got it! Voilà!
I've read the invisible print and agree

to the mission-impossible terms
of your Eternal Returns Policy. No problemo—
deal me in. I'm set to attempt the death-
defying arterial hemoglobin signature
on the perpetual motion sine wave line. Ouch!
This Parker 51 fountain pen of yours
has quite the bite. Sure! Just put one of those
billion-dollar Band-Aids on my tab. I mean,
"It's only money," right? There! Done! So, when
do I begin to rebreathe my rebated sum
total of youthful re-breaths—to feel my ticker
re-ticking its renewed accruals
of updated re-beats? Oops! I'm sorry, ma'am—
my bad. As you say, "All in good time—
all in good time." Oh! And thank you for yours!

Whirling-Dervish-Looney-Tunes-Tasmanian-Devil-Perpetual-Rocking-Double-Z-Poetry-in-Motion-Machine *Me*!

The heaven-sent miracle to all that ails me
daily is movement—muscle, tendon, bone,
ligament, visceral, existential, planetary,
intergalactic, $E = mc^2$
up-down, to-and-fro, kinetic energetic
molecular movement—one atom, cell,
corpuscle, heartbeat, breath, one hominid myth,
science-fiction truth, Sasquatch footstep
after another, as in Let 'er Rip! Go, Man,
Go! Bring it on in spades, Babe! Take that
extra tuck and let each "*Never*-Stop"
stop-watch-second buck! Even in trapeze,
acrobatic sleep, I swing, I flip, I twirl,
somersault, spin, "fly through the air
with the greatest of ease..." always
"rollin', rollin', rollin'..." in *Rawhide* pursuit
of my cure-all, my poultice, anodyne, fix,
my dream-come-real snake oil elixir
cocktail of choice. I guzzle speed—laser-
lit, warp-ten Starship Enterprise, whiplashed
Hadron-Collider-God-Particle speed
by the sloshing black-hole-full. I consume slo-
mo gravity-less asteroid bowling-alley rotation
on steroids. I grab flash-n-dazzle
by its bare ass, gusto by its peach-fuzz
short hairs, pizzazz by its sizzling

comet tail, oomph by its *mama* of all
tuba-band oom-*papas*! I grab hold and hang on
for full-throttled trips into the un-star-charted
farthest-quadrant-reaches of infinity, of Forever
Ever Land, where I'll drink *any* effin' thing
to quench my earthly thirst gone berserk,
anything to kick all seven of my chakras,
my too-numerous-to-count auras,
my endless electric energy fields
into super-action-hero magnum opus mode. *"But...*
how...," I know you're squirming to know,
"do I ever find time to pull the ripcord
on my nitro-fueled funny car's duel
de-accelerator chutes to slow me down
enough to write poetry?" I don't. I just climb
aboard the sharpened-lead-pencil
rocket-ship bronc launching into the wild
word yonder, blasting off with each
bardic clock-tick of my juicy life
as I pluck poems like notes
stolen from The Mozart Zarzyski Orchard
highest nebula of overture fruit I soar through
dripping juicy-sweet with music, me
being merely a single syllable of the purest
jeweled movement of time, ad infinitum!

Getting Rich on Paper

It's as easy as slipping scrolls of blood-
stained poems into Creativity's Infinities
one-way pneumatic tube—as easy
as punching the flashing green neon SEND
button with my left fist
while hoisting with my right
a jigger of Writers Tears Irish Whiskey on ice
to whatever silence is out there
on the receiving end of the crystalline
cylinder. The trick, you see,
is not needing to know
what the career returns are
on your investment, other than the just
reward of letting go, moving on
to the next poem. The goal is to
*un*collect the thick tome
titled "The Collected Works of...," to *un*save
the saved—to live, not *re*live,
write, not *re*write, what has already been
relived, rewritten. And so I deliver
scroll after scroll, a paper carrier
slinging into a blinding blizzard the daily
Globe, Tribune, Chronicle, from sidewalk
to imagined stoop. Thirty-five feet
or thirty-five trillion light-years

deep into the psychedelic
fireworks out yonder, it's all the same
Big Bang silence of non-applause. It is
all the same constant grind
against gravity, the same suction,
the same magic-act gasp
that draws me back to the Intergalactic
Drive-Up Bank, where poetry is worth
however many damn figures I can
cram with my micro-tipped BIC
ballpoint pen to the left
of the decimal on the "No Cash Back!"
deposit slip that reads in big bold
letters capped, **MAY YOU NEVER
QUIT YOUR DAY JOB, BABY!**

Interplanetary Hernia Ultrasound

Simply to make small talk
enough to shatter the sterile din,
I quip to the quite lovely
young woman technician
wanding, just beneath the frontal elastic
band of my zodiac-wheel black speedos,
my axle-greased lower extremities
in the dim-lit room, minus skylight,
on a business-as-usual *for her*
humdrum Monday morn, "Please don't be
alarmed, ma'am, should your screen reveal
anatomical abnormalities
foreign to your trained eye, as I am *not*
from this planet." She, flinch-less,
not missing a single beat, or blip,
replies, "Okay, *so* Mister
Zarz-zin-sky, then what planet is it
that you *do* hail from?" To which I go,
"Planet UniPoet, of the Galaxy
Rocking Double Z, Quadrant **Butte!**,
Universe Zambuddha-Duo." To which she
then goes, "Oh, I see—thank you
for your *special* share. This
explains everything, Mister Zarz-zin-sky
from Planet UniPoet, of the Galaxy Rocking
Double Z, Quadrant **Butte!**, Universe
Zambuddha-Duo. Congratulations! It's a boy!"

Zeke Zarzyski

I. Alarm Clock Dog

You cannot tie a dog up with a chain of sausages.
Jamaican Proverb

Toward clapper ears flapping his "wake-up!"
shake, I stir from curled, fetal, deep-
under-cover warmth on sleep-in Sunday
to reach way too early for the OFF
button—a cold-nosed Big Ben
licking my hand before hot-pawing-it
out the bedroom door, his way of leaving
not one single instinctive scintilla
of canine doubt that it's high time
we get up while the getting is good
to get something done.
                        Let's see your iPhone
Siri roust you with such animated persuasion
out of your exotic tropical island
dream toward sober reality's back door, where,
sporting only your bucking bronco boxer undies,
you greet, like the Abominable Snowman
his-self, thirty-below wind chills
extinguishing your last fading flicker of hope
for REM sleep re-entry, thus prompting you
instead—hell, as long as you're up—to scribble
yet one more zany ditty about your darling dog, Zeke.

II. "*Cookie*-Down-The-Hall" Chaser

Every morning after we "go feed horses"
then fetch the daily paper down the lane,
Zeke Zarzyski anticipates with glee
the final leg of his a.m. trio
ritual his lexicon recognizes as "*Cookie*-
down-the-hall." And not just
any old run-of-the-*Cookie*-mill
Cookie, mind you, but his big
six-inch bone-shaped *Cookie*, which,
if pitched with perfection, will *Cookie*-
tumble over the *Cookie*-colored
ocher shag-napped carpet
up to 10-12 *Cookie* feet
after landing, and come to rest
in one fetch-able *Cookie* piece, *unless*
I blow my cameo role in this
cinematic *Cookie* scene to *Cookie* bits
by ricocheting the fragile tidbit
off the baseboard or doorjamb (*ahhh*, shit!)
where it shatters into what seems to Zeke
a kazillion *Cookie* atoms—both our days
shot and shattering *with it*
before we hardly even get *Cookie*-started.
                                        Thus,
I've learned to fathom that I'm The Champeen
Doggie-*Cookie*-Lobber of the whole
canine *Cookie* cosmos. I take pride in
kicking Zeke's *Cookie*-cuisine day off
on a pantingly-happy note, his breakfast
app-a-teaser coming to a cushiony *Cookie* halt
intact and camouflaged by the butt-ugly

shag from which Zeke will shag
his **Cookie** goody, once he sniffs it out, and *then*
gallop *up* the hall, between my forked
Golden-Arches legs,
around both living room couches, back
full-circle to his favorite **Cookie**-munching
spot on the northwest corner of the Ranch
Oak kitchen table—*unless*
I, right on Zeke's tail-stub, nudge him
around the **Cookie** horn, two, three, even four
more times, leaving us both winded and, way too
early, itching for our afternoon "na-na
nu-nu" when Zeke will yip-yip-
yip in Technicolor-Techni-**Cookie** dreams
(ask my shrink, not me, how I know this?)
of animated acrobatic cartoon **Cookies**
back-flipping, hand-springing, somersaulting,
cartwheeling by the macaroon-
snickerdoodle **Cookie** multitudes
fleeing, for their un-crumbled **Cookie**
lives, from **Cookie**-Monster Zeke
down, down, down the **Cookie**-chasing hall.

III. Australian Shepherd Dump-Run Meditation

Mostly for the love of an old dog
sprawled across the saddle blanket
seat cover of an old pickup—Zeke's
head cradled in a third-gear
lullaby between the wheel and my lap

as I fret his favorite chord
progression down the neck
to his "G-spot," dog-chakra tailbone—we ease
our way over gravel
road the old truck knows so well
by carburetor heart, all it takes
is my two-fingered-steering touch
to keep us cruising in the ruts
true as rails. With our wind-groomed
load of loose hay, woodlot bark,
aspen leaf and lawn duff
rakings settling into a bread-loaf
mound in its box, the Ford hums
along in eight-part harmony as we
three bask in our laid-back
Saturday afternoon ritual. Through this
cumulonimbus-cirrus cloudscape
pantomiming rolling prairie, buttes,
buffalo jump, buckbrush coulee,
crazy quilt landscape, we become the simple
dolphin-swim needlework—in and out
of sight, down into swale up over dale—
each stitch of us, no less
binding of this moment in time
than all the rest. Zeke's wits
roused by a coup-counting owl
swooping over the hood, he sits up
leaning into me like fifty pounds of pure bliss
incarnate. The world outside ours muted,
what more tuned-in essence of life
loved, as it is lived here and now, than this
ascension into the center of western Zen.

My Father, The Southpaw

Right arm in a straight-jacket sling
three days after rotator cuff surgery,
I go to work, full-tilt, no give,
packing firewood, one hefty chunk
head-locked in ol' lefty
per steady-clipped trip—slick-
light-snow-over-glare-ice—
between woodlot and garage
for no sane reason other than to shout
into the dark as loudly as I can
to my deceased hard-rock-miner
lumberjack father, "Thanks, Dad,
for drilling into me this
never-say-die defiance, so deep
it thrives, you thrive, *we* thrive
where death will never
reach us, with either hand."

Modern Medicine

On the first day of spring, twenty seventeen,
I time-travel back to *being*
seventeen, in 1968, when I called the shots
over my lithe, sinewy obedient body
fueled on testosterone, adrenaline, endorphins,
serotonin, oxytocin, dopamine, Pabst
Blue Ribbon, *The Magnificent Seven*
cocktail of juicy musical youth
my jazzed-up bloodstream guzzled
by the lusty gallon straight
out of the high-test-ethyl cast iron nozzle.

Fast-forwarded, *minus* my approval,
a mere two-three eye-blinks of time, *I*, now
hooked up to the Golden Years
drip-bag IV—my inner elixirs
reduced from gully washer
to stagnant slough to mere mud puddle—*I*
find myself demoted from '56 Buick
Roadmaster back seat porn-super-star
to orthopedic surgeon office
front-row penitent begging miracles not
even some sci-fi-god-mafioso-don
hybrid-cross bearded Joe Pesci-
look-alike could ever deliver.

I kiss the sacred copulating constrictor
Caduceus ring of my sawbones, Pope Pike,
as I genuflect on my one

only half-gimpy knee in praise of cortisone,
NSAIDs, stem cells, whole-body-n-brain
cryotherapy, scalpels and sutures, and...
and... "How you getting along these days,
Paul," the doc not so much inquires
as he declares, like Abbott
telling Costello "Who's on first." Testing
his rote with a practiced quip, I fire back,
"More rode-hard-n-put-up-lathered
than a plus-sized naked-lady
inflatable rubber doll at a lumberjack camp
run by the Sisters of Mercy
Timber Company, that's *how!*"

And if Doc Pike thinks *that's* funny,
just wait 'til he opens *my* bill
to the tune of 500 ccs of comic relief
needled deep into *his* crazy bone's
cockamamie joint. That'll teach the young,
buff, former pitching star
orthopedist for not sharing with an old
broke-down rodeo poet from another planet
his Ponce de León secret map
to the Fountain of Youth ditch water
he mixes each night with his top-shelf
bourbon stash, shift-after-Great-Falls-Clinic-shift,
keeping all *his* moving parts
in lubed-up salubrious gear. For now.

Science Fiction Wish

Harness-up the two of us
inside the Equine-Pain-To-Human-Pain
Neuron Transfuser Booth. Hobble me,
ankle-to-fetlock with old Cody.
                              Get set
to transfer, like liquid or electricity,
all of her navicular disease
via vacuum tube, hot wire, cosmic
ray or impulse, via voodoo
stickpin or Vulcan mind-meld.
                              Zap
every cell, every molecule and atom
gone askew. From the one limping sadly—
merely nodding toward the torment's source—
siphon, beam, pipe all pain into a body
who talks the talk of doctors.
                              Prep me
without fret or fanfare. Watch the roan
mare's ears perk toward *my* nicker,
toward *my* neigh, as you flip
all 8 sterling toggle switches
to their vermilion ON positions. Fear not
these sharp-toothed sparks, the blue
smoke plumes fuming between us.
                              Picture her,
after this transmission, gingerly stepping
away from the machine with curious ease,

testing each step as if she might slip
suddenly from lush meadow
back into her nightmare of standstill
jagged footing on black ice.
                    Now, picture me
pendulumed on crutches, perched
like a shrug-shouldered vulture
on a dead limb, knuckles turning purple
as the osmotic pain throbs through
my grip into hardwood grain.
                    Witness the inflamed
tissue gasping its last, shooting down
these cripple sticks into their rubber tips
melting into bubbling viscous pools,
acrid smoke and ash sucked
back into Satan's cindery hole,
time-machine-quick.
                    At long last, picture we
two circling, our winged lope
into musical orbit. Far and away,
do we not soar again to prove
how the imagination, jazzed-up, reigns
supreme? How fantasy seeds the deepest
sanctums of un-hobbled truth
once so, *so* impossible to believe, almost?

The Wild Arrival

They're coming to take me away ha-haaa
They're coming to take me away ho-ho, hee-hee, ha-haaa
To the funny farm
Where life is beautiful all the time
And I'll be happy to see those nice young men
In their clean white coats
And they're coming to take me away ha-haaa.
Napoleon XIV

Two months into rotator cuff surgery rehab,
I torque with both shoulders
to lock into four-wheel-drive the frozen-
greased iron hubs of the '69 Ford
pickup—power steering by Armstrong-
Knee-strong, and a bitch to shift
southpaw, as I bust through December drifts
to relay the shipment of my newly-released CD
between the house and the UPS truck-
not-really-a-truck as much as it is
a low-rent Minnesota ice-fishing shack
on wheels.
        The driver, hopped-up
on a last-stop adrenaline high
after another dark-to-dark-to-more-dark
Christmas-delivery triple-shift,
tosses like sacks of cat litter,
like 50-can cases of Spam, like frozen
road-kill, ten dented cardboard boxes
into the icy pickup bed, as I, glaring,
chawing on my bloody tongue,
fight my insides to keep from screaming, "*Dude!*
them's twenty effin' months of my piss-ant

pathetic poetic life, you doggie-doodoo'd-
brown-uniformed abuser
of the parceled arts, *you!*"
                              So this is how
the *Steering With My Knees* CDs arrived, not
quite to their destination, at the junction of
It's-Only-Stupid-Poetry Road
and Screw-The-Music-Too Avenue,
all downhill from where I live to write,
write to live, beneath the yard light
Pole Star hardly a-flicker, horses nickering
hip-cocked into the thick blizzard
the old truck bucks through
with its 300-pound payload
ballast that I sumo-wrestle
over the back axle, scoot out to the tailgate,
one-arm into the house, where, crowding
the blazing hearth, *finally*, I fingerprint
my lusty approval across
the frigid pages and discs of the first
copy plucked from "Box 1."
                              Sipping my fifth Bulleit
Bourbon neat (everything on ice be damned), oh
how it warms my Nanook-ski-of-da-Nort
cockles to close the book on this stormy
horror story with the most torrid,
delusional, youthfully-fueled,
metaphorical toast I can concoct
on frost-bitten notice: *Cheers!* to the frozen
bones of poetry creaking loose. *Cheers!*

to poetic juices oozing, oozing
musically free in the big
Doctor Zhivago-ice-palace back-seat
master bedrooms of vintage Chevys,
Buicks, Pontiacs, Fords, parked,
revved up on Pabst Blue Ribbon six-packs
wedged against accelerator pedals—
8-bangers, heaters, woofers, tweeters, coil springs
all rollicking erotic to teenagers
Steering With *Their* Knees,
getting it on, by God, in the arctic bardic thaw.

Migraine Hangover—the Agonizing First Smile

It might've been the blinking Christmas
tree lights, too much coo-
coo-cooing of turtle doves, sparkling
sharp nutmeg atop the two brandy-nogs
I drank for lunch. Something
brighter than Salvation
Army bell-ringing jingle-
jingle-jingle at every last frenzied stop
I merrily made
ignited the naughty, not nice, cacophony of
trip-hammer neurons, collapsed,
the capillary lattice in the left
front quadrant of my noggin,
blew circuits, popped fuses, lit a party
pack of Black Cat Firecrackers,
swelled the dewlap below my right eye
like a bicycle tube aneurysm
and left me, ad nauseam, seeing crazy
quilt patterns of patchwork pain
that I, miracle of miracles,
somehow—thanks and Happy Birthday, Jesus—
slept almost off. This morning,
feeling limp as tinsel, moving

gingerly as Kris Kringle
after his millionth chimney, I begin
to rip open the crispy
psychedelic Santa wrapping
around my first gift. All I wish for
this Christmas is the sibilant
white whisper of tissue
unfolding and falling in one
snow-on-snow
slow motion to the muffled plush
nap of frontal lobe—holy,
holy, oh-so-holy, an angel's
downiest kiss upon my brow.

Cigar Box Chocolates

La Aurora Cigarros, petit coronas, the logo
lion resting, its belly filled with dark
rounds, dense pods, domed
nubs in exotic rows, raw
and uncut, gem or drug,
their facets, all heft,
nubile curve and swirl,
aerodynamic aroma of
cacao seed married to maduro
tobacco, their pheromone
cornucopia from the lid
lifted, its hinged flap
like the cover of a Red Grooms *Ruckus*
Chocolate pop-up book
opened close to the jaws, the whirling
dervish vortex
into each pore, follicle, bud,
iris and tympanum—into membrane
left brain, right brain, the secret
gray mazes of anfractuous passages,
into the blood and juices of whatever
unruly demigod humors
make us human,
or not. Pick one. Feel

the ridges of fingerprint
melting, succumbing
to the chocolate's hottest
recollections, black
matte finish leaving
a slick sheen on the lips,
the incisors not cutting, not crushing,
but merely suggesting the shell
collapse, reptilian burst
into the prehistoric, the tongue
deluged with primeval
music, papillae in a mosh pit
of delirium, monastic calm, Cro-Magnon
man romp, succubus gluttony,
banshee primal scream, all
a-roil in one smoldering
scalding cauldron of blood-
hungry roar from below,
rogue endorphins
stalking the euphoric
heart's thicket.

Endorphins

Dream poems, She feels, are little
more than sleight-of-hand mind games,
a simple ruse, an easy maze
in and out. And so the Muse, always
better selfish, stays up late
holding to the day's last
gasp. Forcing Herself
to finally say "so long," She
mourns for all
the words unwritten, the line
that might have shaken free
one purgatory orchard soul. Sleep
as meaningless as poems She can't recall
guiding toward the light last week,
all that ever matters is
tomorrow morning's heart
and lungs afresh—Her "ready"
breath at 5 a.m., Her blood "set"
erotic in the blocks of the inside lane.

Literary Lust, Voyeuristic Love, LAX Theatre

At his gate, waiting for his flight to anywhere,
he beholds the much younger
photograph of himself
grinning from the back-cover dust jacket
of the poetry book, a woman, facing him
posture-perfect in the seat across the aisle,
reads with both hands—the cloth edition
poised higher than a choir
hymnal. Her ring-less fingers, long
religious rays of light, make him believe
she is the most sacred lady
to engage his poetic pleas and promises
since he prayed on his knees
at 15—his girlfriend, three weeks late—
to the Blessed Virgin Mary.
                                  She is a lover
of words, he can tell by the sensual
architecture of her brow, subtle
movements of curve and sweep. He watches
her forehead—aurora borealis
light swirling hypnotically to each slow turn
of the page. Her fingertips tighten,
one of them sliding
with perspiration over the slick
litany of back-cover blurbs
to touch his cheek, the flesh beneath
her manicured nails growing

a deeper pink with each line
she reads. He thinks he knows the poem,
the stanza, the very passage
arousing this fervor. He does not
bow to the impulse to glimpse
her breasts pressed together
under a red cashmere sweater
by her forearms, her sleeves bunched
above elbows braced
to the arm rests. The grain of her is
marbled, sinewy, defined—nourished
by all that is truly feminine.
                          He is tempted
to rise from his seat, take one step and bend
over her to kiss the pellucid white
crescent moon of skin
just inside her hairline, the soft place
where light filters through
to touch delicately the deckled edge
of thought. He vows not to peek
down into the private space
between retina and page, the synapse
across which intimacy races
wishing to become wisdom,
love. He does not need to see
his lines reflected in the lens
of her eyes he believes deep blue

pools of ink, does not need
to be dazzled by the calligraphy of her
lips perfectly fit
to the curvature of his words. His tongue works
the inside of the same cheek
her fingertip just barely nudges now
upon the dust jacket, the deep
pink beneath her nail waning now
as her elbows relax, the book
like heavy velvet burgundy curtain
slowly lowering over the closing scene.

The Body's Most Vocal Gonad

When the Poet bleeds most deeply into the page,
the taste of word-blood is sweetest
to the tongue of those willing and able
to endure reading through the suffering
into the love.

Ground Zero

Hovering in a love ritual, engaged
in lepidopterous play—though who am I
to speak today of frolic or romance—the two
ivory butterflies aflutter
in my lane could not be
mistaken for blossom petals or snow
flakes on this radiant September eleventh
paved straight-away we claim
all to ourselves, plenty of distance and time
to brake, downshift, veer,
were I not blindsided,
traveling at the speed of grief
twenty-one hundred, eighty-eight point three miles
east of Manchester, population 200, Montana.

Transfixed by the televised rubble, focused
on each one of the thousands
stricken, I drive through these winged lives
like thin victimless air, not even
the faintest tick-
tick against the pickup truck's grill,
the final-countdown seconds

of not just any world, but *this*
unswerving world, so muted, so fleeting
in its brief equilibrium, no less
innocent in its spin—
twin buildings, twin butterflies,
these primeval collisions that turn us
eternally into something other.

What Stephen Hawking, the Definitive Poet of All Time, *Might*, As We Speak, Be Coming Face-to-Cosmological-Face With

Only two things are infinite—the universe and human stupidity.
And I'm not sure about the universe.
Albert Einstein

You can no more win a war than you can win an earthquake.
Jeannette Rankin (1880-1973)
Montana Congresswoman

Planet earth is the number one
rated, syndicated half-hour sitcom
showing on Universal Big Screen
Satellite TV. We have become such
natural born comedians, in fact,
that we've, in a mere century, outgrown
our need for the canned-laugh
soundtrack machine. Across the cosmos
intelligent life religiously watches us,
never missing an episode
because a good guffaw or, better yet,
belly laugh—they've known this
ever since something touched
off the mother of all fireworks
extravaganzas—is the only law, rule,
cure, hope, virtue, truth. When someone dies
they join the viewing audience
so fast, they host the hijinks
of their own wake, thus upping

one notch The Sagan Ratings. "Love?"
you ask. "Pain? Happiness? Loss? Despair?
Courage, mercy, faith?" Knee-slapping,
side-splitters all, yet not as slapstick hysterical
as our quest for success, security, status,
concepts so inane, they make black holes
look tangible as frothing pintfuls
of Guinness. There *is* great news,
however, tagged to this revelation
should it leave you distraught. Our world
will never end. We'll be forever
the longest running series
on The Eternity Network. We've become a cult hit
attracting "*Bill*-ions and *Bill*-ions" of devoted
viewers who believe
even our reruns are a riot.

Knock-Knock-Knocking
on Doomsday's Door

*Pollution, greed and stupidity are
the greatest threats to Earth.*
Stephen Hawking

This poem is a flagrant waste
of what little is left of our end-of-days
aboard this page, this space, this time-
bomb orb tick-ticking
hotter by the stopwatch second. Why
squander one fraction of one
single degree of axis rotation
writing or reading this
pitiful drivel, or, sillier yet,
listening to it being read
to us at our final bedside
like some Aesop's Fables last sacrament
fairy tale we strain to believe
will save us from Hades?—
from the boogeyman dark?
                    This poem is *not*
our skydiving heart's nitroglycerine pill
reserve chute, *not* our hidden doom-
and-gloom ampoule of great escape
cyanide, *not* our pearly-gated secret
entryway into the surreal
dreamscape world
of smoked opium. *Nor* is it

our confessional Etch A Sketch
shaking clean of sacrilege
to flightless acts of contrition—slurred
words dribbling like pap
off our chinny-chin-chins
onto the deck of God's Flagship going down,
down for the galactic count of three,
like some torpedoed Noah's Ark,
down into the old cosmic commode,
into the black-hole toilet bowl,
down, *down*, DOWN with chosen-ones us
perched in our steepled wheelhouse,
upon our chosen-one throne,
while choosing not to lift
one chosen-one pinkie off the holy-
water flush lever?
               This poem bites *not*
quite sharp enough its barbed tongue
to keep from frankly asking, "*Why*? Why,
Mother-Earth-Fuckers, were we so
loath to direct instead our genitalia
like pious scientists

pissing in abstinence on the mizzenmast
spiraling up in flames?" *Ahhhh*, screw it—
who can blame the deified
muses refusing to rescue
dunce-capped-stooges
us from our catatonic corner-
gazing selves. Face it—this poem did
not have a prayer in snowballed hell
at putting the kibosh to our atomic
holocaust, the coup de grâce
to our self-prescribed genocide,
the Yosemite Sam "Whoa!,
when I say Whoa! I mean
WHOA!" to this global boiling-over
we choose still to deem a Looney Tunes
"That's All Folks!"
cartoon spoof. This poem may as well be
Wile E. Coyote playing Rooski
Roadrunner Roulette
with all six Acme six-shooter chambers
sporting live rounds!
                  And so, this poem
lampoons its own demise, as it mocks
the lost poet depositing it here
like a fiery paper sack of shit
plopped under cover of darkness

upon the poet's *own* porch. Good! He *is* home
to hear, above the TV scream
of too-real news, his swan song's
loud pummeling
on his bunker's screen door. To hear
the absence of 1950's kids'-prank
snickering to his stocking-footed
stomp into the putrid
flames. To hear even the high-
frequency, death rattle
wheeze of his own petrified lines
gasping their photosynthetic last.
                              This poem,
then, exists only to sift its own ashen
bone-fragment remains
through its own chaliced fingers
raised in a pathetic gesture
of reckoning, raised to the billowing God-
cloud of what was once
each and every miracle, each
and every mystery, each and every
molecule of merciful matter
this poem held dear—of what was
once living, breathing
twice-blest you, me, them, us, it.

Opium Poem Prayer

Darkness warshed over the Dude—darker'n
a black steer's tookus on a moonless prairie night.
*There was **no** bottom.*

Sam Elliott—*The Big Lebowski*

Should I, late in life, find myself
going it alone, on the threshold
of the next teleportal, and about to
step through the interspatial
gateway of six-or-eight-
dimensional time, please may I
do so while inhaling
deeply through an ivory-stemmed pipe
into the silk-paper lanterns
of my buoyantly joyful lungs a bowlful of
The Beautiful Buddha
in a Butte, Montana Song Dynasty
throwback den of yore
doubling as a bordello? Oh, Lord,
all I ask is a painless taste of high
heaven before entering the heavy-
gated lair of whatever
awaits to greet and spirit away
my bullet-riddled P-51
fighter soul
spiraling down, machine guns
smoking, into the fiery side.

Furthur-Bless-America Big-Bang Future-Flashback Boogie

I've enjoyed being a famous writer—except that,
every once in a while you have to write something.
Ken Kesey

On Sunday morning, after the psychedelic
bus rears-up out of the Oregon swamp with a Hi-
Ho-*Furthur*-n-Away into the deepest
cerebral folds of the old cowpoke cosmos,
the woman you love sleeps long past dawn
in her tie-dyed Grateful Dead sweatshirt. Home
last night before the stars even started
to get a buzz on, you escaped the tame,
safe, catered housewarming. You flashed back
past the Comfortable, past the Contented,
the Compromised, the Compliant and Complacent—past
C-stands-for-*average* lifestyle
modifiers, to the *F*ucking-A-*F*ulminating,
*F*earless, *F*ree-as-in-Woodstock-
Richie-Havens-singing-"*F*reedom, *F*REEdom!"
*F*orbidden-*F*ruited '60s. Hungover still
from the Bloody-Maryless '80s and '90s, you scorn
the oxymoron, "young Republicans,"
to end all oxymorons. You'll never forget
your geometrically symbolic youth, the far-out
two a.m. television test pattern
you could have marveled at for decades
turning suddenly to static and snow. Now,
craving to relive your sinful magnificence

into the new millennium, you sit squirming,
determined at your November eleventh desk,
a flimsy window between you and the aspen
flickering not even the shakiest of its last
few neon leaves, like brain cells, still
barely hanging on
after rocking dusk-to-dawn in a rip-
snorter of a Ken Kesey
launchpad wind. Counting down to kingdom come's
wildest-ever animal-loving-plant,
plant-loving-animal, electric bash, you lick
not Starbucks, but Emiliano Zapata-brand
coffee off your mustached lip
like an aphrodisiac
elixir laced with something illicit
and leftist. Your kaleidoscopic mind
keelhauls all that is not
iconoclastic, climbs aboard the next rocket
bronco out and, following the lodestar
known to us as Poetry, lifts you off,
awestruck, into the eternal
fireworks of words.

Boom or Bust but Do Not Trust the Judges:
An Anarchistic, Pugilistic, Metaphorical Musical—
Bush v. Gore Supreme Court Decision, December 12, 2000

The bell sounds loudest between rounds
eleven and twelve. "Do it, or die trying!"
your corner implores, ice water
poured into the front of your trunks
to hone your focus, to zero and tune
you in to the static-less sweet
music of your heart, that rap-beat
rapid-fire backbeat projectile prompt—
"...your *JAB!*...your *JAB!*...
your *JAB!*...goddamnit...your *JAB!*"—
rising like mantras
above the rope-less ring of rhetoric.
                              "Your *JAB!*—
your God's-wrath, Revelations-
most-unmerciful *JAB!* Your *JAB!*, baby—hammer your *JAB!*
like the psalm's stiff antithesis, like the stinging
succinct punctuated strafing epitaph
to all other parenthetical punches,
uppercut to hook—your lights-out,
sweet-dreams-evil-schemes, amen-to-the-end,
radical *JAB!*
              Follow it always into battle,
into the polemical brouhaha. Forget the palooka,
the bum, the punch-drunk-prez-puppet
perpetually smirking, the shellacked
plastic manikin, the literal stool

pigeon across the ring from us. Duck
chicanery, head-fake ruse, feint illusion,
rope-a-dope subterfuge. The most odious
foe is that majority bench of quack judges
dubbed Supreme.
                    Thus, stick it with precision—your *JAB!*—
until their five upper lips thicken
speechless, until ten eye sockets All Rise
like leavened bread. Remember, Lady Justice
beneath her black blindfold
dons the stigmatic dark glasses
of the winner who got robbed
blind in a split decision.
                    And so you
just got to go for the KO, just got to
keep on double-jacking your *JAB!*...your *JAB!*...
home to the nail-head
red welts of the judges' pudgy cheekbones
budding a hematite
hematoma purple
splitting into resinous blossoms
no cutman worth his salt could End-Swell,
tourniquet-pinch, staunch
with sanctimonious salve. The last vestige
of false anthem the fallen will recall

is the rocket's red glare of your
shock-n-awe *JAB!*"

                    Oh sweet science of
Apocalypse Now, Armageddon Never,
Revolution Soon, we snap crisp salutes to
your crescendo of sixteenth-note-fast-
rat-a-tat-tat-scat-song-
one-two-three-fours
tattooing the theocratic
into everlasting retirement. We hail your *JAB!*—
your militant-left *JAB!* That 4th of July
anarchy flashback. That fireworks crack
of your patriotic *JAB!* That Blue, yes Blue,
Angel sortie of thunderous truth
roaring over The People's Coliseum cheer
rising high above the most truthful
silence of the slap-happy gavel-wielders
slabbed on the canvas like cadavers,
VACANCY! VACANCY!
stamped in black-neon on their pop-up-book
perpendicular shoe soles—all five
five-and-dimers cold-cocked,
down for the 10-count, not one
crooked decision "*LEFT!*
LEFT! LEFT!" in their rung bells.

Pussy Riot—*Vagina Dentata*

We "U.S.A! U.S.A! U.S.A!" Trump-dumb-
duped spectator-sport patriots
know not one thing about risking
the synapse between coliseum seats
and gladiator arena, about crossing the thick
red vaginal expanse of political
mine fields—not under cover of lush
jungles of democracy
on a celestial night, but out in the wind-
beaten 80-below persecuted open. I'm not
talking erotica from the Muse, Erato—no
sex kitten genitalia, no triple-X
porn. I'm talking the female heart
as the body's most vocal gonad
incited not so much by the heat
of passion as by the Siberian
freeze of tyranny. As for our Grunge,
Metal, Psychobilly, Rap, Gothic Rock,
Hip-Hop, Christian Punk, Funk...*Fuck*
the cloistered American noise
of we, the pap-fed complacent, seldom bearing teeth
enough to bite for change, to pound home
loud with reckless abandon to the soul
those powers of music so perilous
its players must scream through gallows hoods
the bravest anthems ever prayed.

Loving the Mamba

High school lovers out on ambush,
crouched behind the Model A
rusting among apple trees, the aught-six
loaded, they petted and necked and did not notice
darkness and the black
bear they'd come to kill
lumbering toward them, a funnel
cloud through the tall wild hay
between orchard and forest canopy
holding the night, the bear,
tunneled in coolness
until now. They froze
to the hypnotic side-to-side
swinging of its head
behind the vertical crosshair, its nostrils
working to scent,
through ripe Winesaps and Russets,
the blood they lusted for each month.

They backed off, turned tail and ran,
his first love in her red, hooded sweatshirt
gliding like a cardinal through dusk,
and him, fingering the Winchester's hair trigger,
covering their flank. Through creek bottom
clotted with alder and popple, they clawed

their way through jungle, felt cold
eyes tracking them—the predator-turned-prey
quick switch, maybe a split-second
glimpse of Vietnam. Or the apocalyptic fire
and fear of their impending head-on collision
while coming home after losing
to Spruceville—no gridiron heroes,
no pom-pom hurrahs from cheerleader
sweethearts in the 4-banger Scout. They swore
every wetness was blood
until they learned how blood glimmers
blacker than anything fluid
moving under moonlight, the highway
sequined with windshield fragments—
scale-glitter off the black
mamba—and that glimmer
shellacked over a buddy's face in shock.

All of this—hatred of rival teams,
vicious hitting in the trenches,
trap and cut-back blocks, the ambush
they set for bear
that tracked them through thicket
back to their car, the crash,
buckle and jagged shredding of steel,
axles snapped like bones,

smoldering shrapnel and flesh and her
swerving out of love and leaving
him to wake alone, years later, to cold sweat
flashbacks, that wetness in the dark—all of this
the closest he has come to knowing
how a soldier, run amok in dead-of-night
hand-to-hand, might believe all women
look erotic in black—shameless lamia
dressed wicked for the kill—as he is
making his crazed love to the enemy.

The Pedophile Priest Enters the "Wanted: Dead, *Not* Alive" Prayerless Lair Confessional of His Prey

Down on altar-boy knees
bruised, we pleaded not to have to
serve the 6 a.m. mass with you—prayed
to *your* oblivious God,
prayed until our souls bloated, until,
wringing-wet with night-sweats guilt,
our faith festered into carrion
under the enormous weight of prayers
ignored.
                    Fifty years since, the demons, still
feasting, shit their seething hosts
bit-by-fiery-bit to parasitic cinder. God
damn your feigned "mea culpa." God damn
your "Father, Son, Holy Ghost," sign of the cross
mockery, your confessional tallies and tolls
of sins, of victims—your John Doe
toe-tagging of the sacrificial dead.
                                        Butcher
block meat upon that sacristy table
where you desecrated the innocent, is how
I still picture Satan's lackeys finding you
in bloodied cassock—the bowie knife
Scotch-taped inside my boot
chafing my ankle raw

as you placed "The Body of Christ"
upon the defiled tongue
of your prey kneeling before you, vengeance,
not the Lord's, but *mine*,
honed-in on the predator heart:
                              "Thou shalt not
kill," not kill, *not* kill, *unless...*
chanted my 5th commandment caveat—*unless*
thine ear is pressed
into the black cloth, forced toward the drum-
beat that metes out the blood
arming with lust
the Wicked One's bunker.
                              You seek
pity? Acquittal? A crisp, clean bill
of ecclesiastical health? Sorry, Padre,
wrong door. The Vatican
cannot afford your bail—no
Paraclete sanctuary in paradise,
no overnight trafficking of a fugitive
"black-n-white" to his fresh parish
this time around. Your "three Our Fathers,
three Hail Marys, go and sin no more"
venial penance doled out

ad nauseam in monotone rote
does not undo the diabolical—your Latin
Act of pseudo Contrition,
pisses with your *"Dominus vobiscum"*
into our vindictive wind.
                              We, the wounded
for life, do hereby sentence *you* to life,
to our life, life minus the beauty of one lit
respite from eternity's black
wet oubliette. Because Our Father has yet
to "deliver us from evil"—because
evil, rather, has been delivered back *to* us—you
so aptly have strayed
into the wrong sacrament. You have stepped
instead into your last rites
deathbed stood on end, the unctuous
stench of your sanctimony
sealed here for good.
                              Into this suffocating
dusk, you too now, snuffed,
hyperventilating your dying
plea, will perish with the last votive
candle's fading puff of smoke. Your casket,
lined in lead, lashed in chains,
is the tight-fisted rosary,

beaded with padlocks
arc-welded shut by the forgotten
gods of karma. Ironworker gods. *Our* gods.
Gods unafraid to look down, to see, to bow
in shame to the centuries of names—sacred
names, saintly names, forsaken names,
the skeletal remains of names still
shackled to the walls of the papal
vaults, names up in flames—his name,
her name, faceless names, *our* names...David, John,
Michael, Joseph, Matthew, Mary...Paul...

Ars Poetica Kevlar—The APK-26 Bullet-Proof Poem:
Upon Carrying "For Life" the *Wall Street Journal*
Sandy Hook Mass Shooting Pictorial
Page, "Shattered Lives"

What worth are the poet's words
scribed upon thoughts-and-prayers gauze—
cotton, bamboo, hemp, jute—mere pulp
too soaked to clot and stanch
the temple's stained glass
platelets shattered, spilling at the whims
of invincible ballistics?
                What long-shot odds
mere body-and-blood still face
in the wakes of AK-47, of AR-15,
unabbreviated bursts, if not for this quixotic
willingness to will our A-to-Z-
26-letter alphabet, head-to-toe,
impenetrable—the poem's thin syllables,
sinewy filaments, microscopic fibrils
polymerized, twisted, woven, knit,
clenched tighter than a million fists
spun from the spinneret page?
                    Part myth,
part wizardry, scripture, sci-fi...*why not*
sanctify as supernatural
this futuristic cure to the cancer

of lead—metastasized,
horizontal onslaughts of lead
flatlining we-the-faithful
joy-riding the salvation train
we-the-faithful board day after day
for safe passage?
                    Why bother otherwise
synthesizing our choirs of lines
if not to believe this alchemized song
stronger than the speed of evil,
if not to believe its chemistry
flexed, its tensile-strength-to-weight
ratio, its so-called "tenacity"
fifty-five times that of steel?
                    In other words,
let us now fill our pages with these
inked second skins, these full-body-tattoos,
these sheer, armored leotards,
sheathing us from our own
prosaic law, from decades of bullet-
riddled dirges, patriotic requiems,
sentimental anthems. Let our musical

poetic suits of chain mail DNA,
of molecular bugle calls, of maternal
psalms deliver us from all
future, present, *past*
tragic headline news amended here
for good: "Ricocheted Lead
Returned to Senders—No Victims
Smiling Childishly Below."

Because I Vow in Blood to Burn

The Poem is the landscape upon which its inhabitant,
the Poet, navigates via unmapped words.
And landscape, being more seasoned always than its inhabitants,
knows far more about the Poet's destination
than does the Poet.

Winter Solstice 10-Count

My favorite coffee mug from the dish rack,
six a.m., is so solstice-cold
a corner man could use it as an End-Swell
on his blind fighter, Mr. Magoo, looking like
he's whispered nectarean hive-jive into the ear
of a yellow jacket nest. Is it obvious
I've watched too much inane TV? Can you
tell I stayed awake until two
awestruck by the documentary
footage of Muhammad Ali—stayed up late
mostly to stoke the wood fire, mostly
to save on propane costs, mostly to make sure
December twenty-first did not stick
around one stop-watched round longer
than its allotted time, time
easily freezing in these wind-chills
with their eighty-below reach, weighing in
as this year's pound-for-pound baddest
of the heavyweight bad?
                                        Ten days and counting
the ticks to victory, I'm fixed on Ali poised
buoyant against the ropes, the greatest
premiere of ring wizardry
displayed ever in the coliseum of sweet science
that hot morning in Zaire, fierce
George Foreman punching himself out,

Ali absorbing a pummeling so sinful
no unholy man could stand up to it
on this or any other gravity-riddled planet
a-spin.
        Nineteen hundred and eighty-eight is
fighting for wind, its jaws unhinged,
its legs like vermicelli, no sauce
left to its wicked jab, no *al dente* in its
uppercut or garlic in its hook, no brisk
boil of overhand rights. I sandbag the braggart,
bide my time and plant my left foot
for the parting of the wave. I temper
every day's doom with a palooka poem
animated in my head, bruised in its cocoon
of red leather. My plan is everlasting. *Dance.*
As composed as winged eighth notes
sailing out of the cartoon blue, I will *dance,*
dance through the tsunami's wall, land
my solid one-two-three-four
combination and then, bowing toward love, tower
above the canvas aftermath like Ali
over Liston, over Foreman—Jackson Pollock
caught in a still-shot, lifting his brush
bleeding into another abstract
fractious year's last, long, loving stroke.

Life So Far

The sun chins the horizon
like a gold-medal winner, high
on serotonin, on adrenaline, on the verge
of shattering the galaxy's record
nonillion-rep score. Until today
I have been cooling down for too many years,
losing my fury—dozing off and going soft—
bullshitting the apathetic so-called "fans"
around me until I've become one of them, hoisting
our nosebleed-seats plastic cups of flat suds
day in, day out.
                    The plot is to make us
leave the coliseum forever and piss away
what's left. The hotdog man tempts us,
smothered between health and old age,
with his bark—"Top jobs! Bennies!
Git yer red-hot top jobs with bennies"—
to keep us buying, did he say "goods?"
until the day we punch out. As we count
our change, the hotdog man becomes a speck
in the lower deck. "Where the fuck's
the mustard?" I wonder, as the fat ladies
—their pointy elbows pinning me on both sides—

threaten to sing if I do not stop
yelling "down in front" to the young studs
still fired-up and focused on the games. That was me
before, distracted, I joined the humdrum
ranks of the automaton cloned. I'm weary
of this role—of being cast
an extra to the extras among the extra
throngs needed to make this biblical epic, all glitz
and Hollywood shtick.
                              Today I vow to fight
my defiant way back onto the starlit field,
to master the sun's techniques, to learn
how it grips the bar with fingers
we never see—what muscles it flexes
to vault its slow-motion handstand
across the sky. I want to live
its intricate physics, the aerodynamic
mechanics of strength. Does it kick its legs
for thrust? Does it grimace with eyes closed
below the bar? Because I vow in blood to burn, I will
do my roadwork in the boneyard—
shadowboxing my own stone.

Dying to Live Like Hemingway

"A man can be destroyed but not defeated."
Santiago—*The Old Man and the Sea*

No longer risking my neck in arena theater wars
aboard rodeo horses, I charge at first light's
silent reveille through a drape-less pane
this notebook's blank page, foreboding,
bellicose, strong as the bronc's
shoulders locked for the kick. I'm drilled
most days heart-first into the dirt. But
during that rare dawn when I'm tapped off—airborne,
in tune, in time, in rhythm and sync—line-for-line,
jump-for-black-marlin-jump, I spur the words
vertical across the salty chop
to the bullring's bravado and salvos of *Olé!*
and bulges of muscular dust. On those mornings,
I die to live like Hemingway,
posed in a photo arm's-reach from my desk—Hem
grinning like a grandee, his black cabochon eyes
deep-set beneath his Stetson's brim, two
rainbow trout hanging, one grappled in each hand, poised
off his hips like matched ivory-gripped pistols
notched. Papa, my paladin, my patron
matador saint of romance and brutal youth,
you were right. What life, less our sirens—
minus the fire of visceral sin, of instinct,
fiction, myth—is worth further journey

upon last-chapter earth. *What life,*
without the burning swirls of mermaids
luring us deeper, deeper
into the moon's reflection, into the moon's music
on mute—their vernal world,
our lucky polestar, only just barely
always out of reach of our foolhardy lines.

Two Takes on What's Left:

I. Toward My Sixties—Letting Go Into Thin Air

At age 55, I testify early,
ahead of deadline, how, going it alone,
I can do my world of words a good turn
on my way out. I've had it
all wrong, touting poems
I *might* write in the fourth quarter
as counting double toward some grand finale
tally, some literary fairytale score. Vice
versa, I say now. My thirties and forties
of my second quarter, lord it
over the first and, so far, third—over
static ticks of the poetry clock's
big and little hands straining
to make it through that most radical arc and up
onto number 9's horizontal shelf
where false hope reigns sublime.
                                    The true free-
soloing poet climber, for the beatific
sake of the last readership vestige
here on earth, relaxes his grip,
lets his claws—clenched to pen, to sheer granite face—
again become mere fingers
opening into blossom all at once,

both hands lifting, buoyant with peace,
above the piano keys in that instant
when the vanishing last note
is banked, secured, preserved
eternally in some musical
humankind vault. Into my swan song
most exalted, I will also fall
free, unexhausted, eyes-shut-tight,
through a dignified abyss of silence—the kiss
goodbye without one dying word.

II. Chutzpah! Count *Up* Not Down! Never Say "Die!"

Waking to a blizzard-withered November
twenty-fifth, two-thousand-six,
wind-chilled thirty-below
Montana daybreak, *who's* got gonads, gall,
gravel enough to plod up to my door
and say to my red face "no way,
never happen," while I'm here
crowing into this bright white moment in time,
tempo, tenor, and temperature—here
crowing my 55.5 year-old
age as merely my midway
mile marker on the black-arced
trajectory through life. *Who?* Nobody. Not one
living, dead, or resurrected
S.O.B., *that's who.*
                Thus, I,
with every atom of gusto'd matter
these young lungs can muster, yell
my one-hundred-n-eleven mantra
countering Old Man Winter's
rimy-breathed "...ashes to ashes
dust to dust..." hoarfrost choruses
out of the north. I chant, I cheer,
"*ONE-ONE-ONE! ONE-ONE-ONE!* Triple ones

or bust! Triple ones or bust!"
                    You goddamn
right, Sugar, on this frigid morn, that's how
my jump-started heart, merely half
way into the eternal curve
called "life on earth," gets high
on the sturdy centrifugal inertia
spinning us like a carnival ride
convexly wild into the next
and final round—that's how my psyche
closing in on its midlife *non*-crisis,
throws itself a 55.5-year surprise party.

Deep Hidden Meaning, Deep Hidden Morning on Mute

Letter by penciled letter, graphite,
biting into the cellulose
molecular make-up of lined notebook paper,
amplifies almost too much
Stratocaster guitar clamor. Window slid open,
not one syllable, not one decibel, not one
sixteenth note trickles through
a single square of screen
mesh above this desk. Insect wings
do not flit. All avian pastorales
cancelled, aspen leaf lenticels yawn
on fixed stems. The acrobatic
second hand, abandoning its steadfast
cartwheel laps around the track,
tiptoes in slippers
above the cotton batten
clock face—time no longer
of the essence. In this tick-less,
bark-less, chirp-less, lawnmower-less
monolithic dawn, what greater
veneration of each heartbeat
shushing the blood

entering the cathedral's nave, what
higher praise of every pious breath
genuflecting with awe into the light,
than to take note, tranquil
note, of this thin smoke
of words, this inaudible whisper,
flameless, with nothing at all lofty to say.

A *"Buon Compleanno!"* Phone Call to Mom

(November 20, 1999)

Living mostly in the wistful, at times whimsical,
shadows her memory left behind,
my mother, two weeks after her stroke,
tells me in Italian "*tutto passa,*
everything passes, *tutto passa*"—tells me
she no longer has the *volontà*
to cook and to bake, her two true loves
my entire life. "What if it's no good?"
she frets. "At my age, it's a sin
my children aren't here to help stuff the bird
for Thanksgiving."
    "It's the original sin
of your original dressing," I console her. "I'll bet
it's Catholic, too, because it too is guilty of being
the best ever, Mom, since those pesky Protestants
docked at Plymouth Rock—not one jar of *giardiniera*
on board. Lucky their Indian brethren
welcomed them at all, after that insipid
pickle relish they passed off
as feast-day fare. Just try to tell me Christ
didn't summon-up an apostolic pint of *antipasto*
at *His* potluck!"
    "Oh, Mom, just pour yourself
a *cicchet* of Christian Brothers
to soothe your *cannarutsi*—
your vocal cords or tonsils or whatever it is
you oil-up enough to sing along with Frankie
Yankovic's 'You can have her, I don't want her,

she's too fat for me,' polka. If you can remember
those goofy lyrics, you can remember
to remember to turn the damn oven on
this year, Mom! And yes, I swear, I promise,
I'll go to confession for swearing."
Trivial
as they sound, these little gifts are
what I give my mother
for her birthday, a million memories away—
silly laughs, feeble promises, and, gift-wrapped
in the plain white paper of this free verse
poem so alien to her canzonetta ear,
a few old-country words I conjure up
from childhood, Mom's heyday—all it takes
to keep two Italian hearts marching,
marching always toward the *appassionata mangia!*
mangia! beat of the next big meal.

Tregiovo (Northern Italy) / Mom's dialect:
  Buon Compleanno!—Good (Happy) Birthday!
  tutto passa—Everything passes
  volontà—Will, volition
  giardiniera—A spicy relish of pickled vegetables in vinegar and / or oil
  antipasto—In northern Italy, a vegetable-olive-mushroom-tuna-sweet
      pickle-etc. medley in a marinara-like sauce preserved / canned in jars.
  cicchet—(chi-kedt)—A shot glass
  cannarutsi—(kan-nah-root-si)—(colloquial?), Throat / Tonsils / Vocal cords
  appassionata mangia!—Eat with passion!

Ink Still Wet

Oh, what ballet, what sway and sinew
of musical movement, as I hang my wash
on five woven-wire lines, on the horizontal
staff, like notes, like words,
like a wardrobe of sound—bath-towel
nouns, dish-towel vowels, blue-jean
gerunds, shirt verbs, modifier socks,
tablecloth consonants and my unmentionables
soaking the September sun into twill,
thread, fiber, stitch, thanks
to cotton pouches bulging
with the most intricate invention of all
evolved pre-n-post iPad time,
the clothespin, the *iPin*!
                              Yes, thank you,
dear patron saint of whittlers,
for these deep-notched pinchers
slipping so snuggly over
overlapped corners of even
the thinnest linens gripped
against stiff wind. Or, more dramatic
than wind, Comanches prodding us
cowpuncher kids to run the gauntlet, wet
towels plastered to our faces
and stretching the lines that snapped

us, grass-stained, to our Levi'd fannies
before those wooden clothespins of yore
would ever turn loose.
                             How simple
it is still, at 61, to rekindle the 1950's
TV mimickings, while pirouetting
a red, western bandana, a "wild rag,"
from Mom's wicker basket to the line—
this pinning of words
into their rhythmic syntax. Yes,
because the 1960's Maytag dryer belt
finally spit the bit. But also because
an Indian summer sun bid me
to go for its magical spin
on these time-machine lines that beam
me back to my mother
singing in Italian, so alive
while folding her Monday loads—
as I'll fold mine, once the ink dries.

Because, Dear Elizabeth Dear,

life is a child's kaleidoscope,
spiraling with phantasmagorical
fantasyland pinwheels,
taking us on its magic
carpet ride odyssey, Turquoise,
New Mexico to Sapphire, Montana,
aboard its Eye Dazzler
Navajo rug in psychedelic flight
at the speed of creative light. *That's* why
I write, as you kid, my "little poems,"
why *this* little poem cheers you on
to paint again big canvases,
from your color wheel palette
swirling with the joyful
oils and acrylics you first stirred
as a girl in the Jemez Mountains
on the *Rio de las Vacas.* Take us back
to those Indian-Cowboy winds
whispering through ponderosa,
through the gambrel-roofed log house
upstairs bedroom window screens, like scrims
of your dream-world musical. Paint us *both*
this time into that enchanted life, two fine,
sable-haired brush strokes

abstract on that grand expanse of landscape—
newborn foals nursing, riffles purling,
Uncle Smitty, Aunt Johnnie, pet deer, Squeaky,
at play in the West. Paint us together in that
granddaddy stand of cottonwoods you sang to,
their open arms spilling over with heart-
shaped notes, each silvery-green leaf
sparkling with what we will always call
"one true love" shining into the wild July
light of a 1950's penny valentine moon.

Living Poetry

Down the echo-chamber hallway
from kitchen to my writing niche
filled with screaming
hurricanes of words
through the window screen, I catch wind
of my wife cooing, cooing
baby talk to our Aussie dog, who,
pushing the century mark,
rediscovers puppy comfort
in the long-voweled, two-syllabled
emasculation of his name
over the hard consonant
handle, Zeke, making him
feel Spike or Duke
unneutered pit bull macho
in his canine prime. "How's sweet
little *Zekey* doing today? Is he hungry
for his *Zekey* food? Does *Zekey* want
to go feed horses? Play
Cookie-Down-the-Hall, go walkies,
go pee-pee poo-poo? Oooooo,
Zekey's such a good dog." I smile,
put my pencil down, close my notebook,
slide the window shut, the wind's words

slamming face-first into the pane—
piling up and melting
against the house like hail
stones horizontally out of the south. I
sit back in what was once
my writing chair, relax my hands,
fingers loosely tongue-n-grooved
in my lap like an old Italian
woman praying her rosary
at High Mass. I close my eyes, listen,
hear again the osmosis of poetry
seeping into the log-walled soul
through its most organic door
opening like the cover
of a book—not one bit less a book
minus a single printed page.

Rolling the Piano Dice Ivories

Why do we choose never too soon
to break cadence? To drift
away from the Vegas
crapshoot delusions of life
as we have chanced them
the whole of our long gamble
across blackjack-table earth? And why
do we shun suddenly the Wall Street
*in*equities of heaven, their vagaries
their futures, stacked against us
with slot machine odds
every roulette wheel spin of the way? Simply
to think otherwise, that's why—not so
much to pencil out losses, to count
our few coup, to cook the books,
to return to Monopoly's GO
where we have already inhaled
each stale molecule twice
in preordained order. But
rather to ferret out fresh notes,
unearth never-before-learned riffs
to songs we yearn to play
on mystical instruments—the sitar

perhaps, or shofar, theremin,
didgeridoo or zither. We move to breathe
to a new groove, where we, forever, are
addicted to *here*, right *here*,
here in this beautiful musical
we have come to call
The Infinity of Now.

Fatherless Father's Day

Everything happens somewhere between
a snail's pace and the speed of light
over years of time counting down
to just one cosmic clock-tick
on the stopwatch of grief. What more
can a son who loved his fisherman father say
on this festive June day with no one
to call on the phone, when all the lines
and towers, earth to eternity, are down
in the aftermath of one biblical
storm of sorrow making heaven, hell,
Armageddon, feel, to an orphan,
far more far-and-away mythological than,
say, a "magic dragon" who "lived
by the sea," or even a mystical,
"fisher of men," who likely is not,
missing wishing His old man
"Happy Father's Day!" again this year, or *is* He?

Cemetery Fireflies—Chiaroscuro

Floating over the smooth marble-
walled pages of the living
rooms of religion—counterclockwise,
always counterclockwise—
fingertips feel high and low
for the long-shot-in-the-dark
theological socket
marked "Death's Outlet"—
a million manicured nails
polished to a high gloss
phosphorescence
sweeping up onto not even one
gently-beveled
electrical-plated
brailled hope of maybe
plugging this lifetime's blindness
into whatever black-hole
swallower of all
vanishing dances of light
leaving us blank, looms next.

Light Warm Life, Dark Cold Death

Willing to weather the relentless
onslaught of eternal absence
nine years after Dad's death,
seven since Mom's, I coast into the cold
wet cemetery at dusk, unlit
save for the few scattered graves
aglow with the faux-celestial
solar lights not yet interred
beneath October snow. Deep into this dark
swallower of sound and silence alike,
I place my faith in the engine's drone,
in the microcosmic grace of sunshine-
deprived eyes in the night—one to the left
for southpaw Leonard, the other,
right, for divine Delia—just barely
flickering to each side of their stone,
to each side, north and south,
of their front porch, four minutes after
I accelerate out through the wrought
iron gates.
        Back to my childhood home,
Mom and Dad's sanctum of sixty years,
these two brighter lights invite me, Paul,
Patron Saint of the Uber-Sentimental,
to recall my folks, perpetually chilled,

winter-after-brutal-Wisconsin-winter,
basking in their 505 Poplar Street
Tahiti-beach bonfire heat. Thus, I spare not
one hard, cold, inherited simoleon
to stoke their tropical memories
warm in an empty house,
thanks to the neighbors keeping tabs
on the colossal lung of the new gas furnace
exhaling on cue, all praise,
all kudos, to old Thomas A. Edison,
to his petite bulb, this tiny life
beside the big-assed thermometer—this light
holding vigil in the living-room window
I still see Mom and Dad peering through,
eyes lit with sadness as I drive away.

Close Calls, Near Misses, Birth, Death, and the Poetic Interstitials

Fifty years after what should have been
my teleportation to the chaotic beyond—I,
hormonally drunk on a purple motorcycle
accelerating off the gravel into the black-
veiled Highway 51
blind-curve trajectory
whistling its shrill incoming
pitch right through me—"fifty years after"
and, let's guess, five hundred or so
poetic progeny later, a mule deer doe
lights out of the gloaming shoulder
into my I-25 straight-away lane
like one more wild reminder: dusk, dark, dawn,
full moon or high noon, babe,
we die or live at the reckless whims
of hit-n-miss long-shot odds, of dumb-luck
toss of crap table ivories
haphazard as asteroids
tumbling, destination-less, through space
like infinitesimal glimpses of what
once was, of what now is, but never of what is
coming next. Screw fate and its second
cousin twice-removed, faith. Screw
the soothsayers, prophets, augurs. I choose to pull out
all the stops, shoot the moon, go all in
on speed-of-light chance
reflex—foot to brake, hand to horn,

wrench of wheel, torque of handlebars,
or the slick-hooved pirouetting toe-
hold of a ballerina deer
lifting off the pavement stage
dropped out from in under time-
stood-still. And if my bungee-tethered soul
does, sometime soon, break free
as it trips the nickelodeon
silent-picture-show switch
to a flickering lifetime of poems
passing right before my bloodshot eyes
slammed shut, then let this poem be
the finale curtain-closer of the five-hundred-
something frames fading to black—*if,*
and only *if,* that is, anyone out there actually *is*
keeping track of all that is not matter.

Poetry—off Radar, with Faith, into the Sacred

*"Truth is like poetry. And most
people fucking hate poetry."*
                    The Big Short

It no longer holds up to the light—
the old saw about poetry being meant
to be read aloud. By whom? Says who? *We?*
We who have failed such euphoric
musical genuflections to Mother
Earth, Brother Sky, Sister Universe,
Father Time, Uncle God? What graces
have we set free? What coat-of-arms wisdom
have our souls borne in courage
to starburst galaxies of words,
words hijacked in transit
to holier places, to holier beings
than are we, the self-anointed
chosen? Let us now otherwise pray,
plead in private, for our very own R.I.P.
"Resurrection Into Poetry:"
                    Lord, may I
humbly deliver, unsullied, these lines
synapsing through me in search of truth,
super-human truth, to wherever is
their higher lure. Screw the literati
cognoscente's stamp of approval
in ink. Screw false audience,

social media's abbreviated thought
of abbreviated souls. Screw applause,
screw all awe other than the poet's own
soaring off this orb's radiant green-
screened page into the glory-be
unknown, into the reckoning
silence above the noise, the noise,
the pitiful noise of the human
voice, where all lies writhe in wait.

Death of the Muse

And when the poetry is finally past
Yes, the world will still last and last and last...

Albeit a little differently than it did before
Minus that one bright shining door
Thrown open raucously at birth
As I chanced upon the magic powers of this earth
With all Her lights, Her darks, Her glories
Her nonillion lives, *Her* noisy stories...

The sun will rise to a nameless dawn
And it's then I'll know something good is gone.

Going It Alone

The secret of a good old age is simply
an honorable pact with solitude.
                    Gabriel Garcia Marquez

Not just for the metaphorical hell of it
but instead, here and now, for good reason,
while peering into this macro-lens
windshield, I think of Amelia's
Lockheed Electra, of Dick Hugo's Buick
Skylark, of everything falling
inevitably through the surrealistic
filter of cumulonimbus—heavy
weather swirling into focus
as first my father, then my mother,
slipped into their final silences. I,
with no sane way out of this
mortal storm, this viscid
mythological maze of biblical
ebb and flow, have come to see
why I never again will thrive
as once I thrived in the same
exact triangular time
with Mom and Dad. Thus, alone,
I embrace the wild
disorder, the metamorphosis, this life
sentence amidst the faithful. No longer
just one more fading pin-tip
blip upon the radar screens
of the gods, I, in solo flight,

am swallowed into the welcoming black-
garmented arms of the dark, far
beyond the blurred
purgatorial borders between
heaven and earth—my cargo of light
grown brighter, pulsing with all
the hope, all the fear,
one disappearing soul can hold.

Her Heart-Mind-n-Soul Holy Trinity

Of all the arts, music is arguably the most potent
in its capacity to elicit responses that best define us as human.

In 1999, I was prompted by the Western Folklife Center to write a short piece, which I titled "Grace," for the National Cowboy Poetry Gathering millennial poster. Twenty years later, asked by the Great Falls Symphony Orchestra and Symphonic Choir Music Director, Grant Harville, to quill a "lyric" in celebration of the Choir's 60th anniversary, I chose to employ a slightly revised version of "Grace" as an opening verse, which then evolved, blossomed, into an "orchestration of sound and image," to which Maestro Harville composed the music. As I'd emphasized in the prologue scribed for the program booklet, "Grace" is both stanzaic poem *and* verse, chorus, bridge song—in praise of Mother Earth and all the choral voices of all Her soulful children, animal and plant alike, paramount of whom, Her kindred sisterhood of women. Our composer-poet-symphony-choir collaboration was performed on December 8, 2020. I consider those 25 minutes of musical time-n-space, set in the Mansfield Theater of the Great Falls Civic Center, one of the highest and most humbling poetic distinctions of my creative life.

Grace

In the soft low light up high
where love has always thrived and will
forever yearn for the colorful hover—a brush stroke
of words out of the West—we still want
free life, we still want fresh air.

And as the millennia meander by
like birthdays to the Earth, what thrill
Montana, wild with her four-legged folk,
still brings us on our daily jaunt
across the land, our daily poem, our prayer.

    Oh give us a home, where the poetry roams
    to our Symphony-of-the-Divine—
    with its stars all in tune to the Bucking Horse Moon,
    to the Milky Way Belfry wind chimes.

    Oh give Earth Her song She will sing eons long,
    Her grace note She'll hold to infinity—
    Her psalm to the light, arioso in flight
    with Her heart-mind-n-soul holy trinity.

    To a woodwind sunrise, birds rhapsodize
    with Her heart-mind-n-soul holy trinity.

II

In the moon glow off fresh snow
where the seeds of music grow and soar
to *Doctor Zhivago's* "Lara's Theme"—a wolf-howl
hallelujah to the night—we give praise
to every sacred voice of Earth's high choir.

And as the mighty strings poise their horsehair bows
to the maestro's gold baton, what roar
icy silence sings between the pines who prowl
with hope for notes of peace, who raise
their arms to virtuoso truth much higher.

> Oh give us Big Sky, let us *all* learn to fly
> to the Chorale Cantata Divine—
> with its stars all in tune to the Bucking Horse Moon,
> to the Milky Way Belfry wind chimes.

> Oh give Earth Her song She will rock eons long,
> Her grace note She'll lilt to infinity—
> Her hymn to the light, arioso in flight
> with Her heart-mind-n-soul holy trinity.

> Percussion's love child, the brass riffing wild
> with Her heart-mind-n-soul holy trinity.

Let this be
Our poem to the Cheyenne "Moon
When The Wolves Run Together"
Our prayer to the Lakota Sioux "Moon
When The Deer Shed Their Horns"

Let this be
Our poem to the Arapaho "Moon
Of The Popping Trees" popping
Our prayer to all of "Nature's People"
Ol' Charlie Russell's West has 'ever borne.

III

In the sunlight's rays graced down
on our green life, our every breath, on all
the eco-notes of this romantic masterpiece—our heart beat
mantras of harmonic brio—oh what blood
we drink, what clean water makes our wine.

And as we renounce the fury, applaud the sound
of life's immortal music, what call
we heed to Mother Earth who sings sweet
Her canzonettas brought to bud
by graceful rains that make Her children shine.

Oh give us deep space, its fire-n-grace,
the Musical Universe Divine—
with its stars all in tune to the Bucking Horse Moon,
to the Milky Way Belfry wind chimes.

May the Goddess of Song hold eons long
Her grace note embraced to infinity—
Earth's anthem to light, The Diva in flight
with Her heart-mind-n-soul holy trinity.

Woman*kind* shined into Beethoven's Ninth
by this heart-mind-n-soul Earthly Trinity.

Woman*kind* on the rise, *Her* Joy glorified
by this heart-mind-n-soul Earthly Trinity.

In the soft low light up high,
where grace will always thrive,
our prima ballerina, Earth,
pirouettes to each poetic word,
each note, each *turn* She sings to spin and spin
and spin into infinity—amen...amen...amen...

Dedications, Acknowledgments, Genuflections...

Dedications

A good number of the poems in this collection, did not "go it alone," but rather were accompanied by the spirit of friendship and/or commemoration as follows:

Dad in the Canopy: *To My Father, Leonard*
Vigil: *To Quinton Duval*
Click...Click...: *To Gordon Stevens*
Starling Seeing Stars: *To Pamela Brown*
Woodnotes To The Churchgoing Woodcutter:
  To Sara Walsh and To Julia Butterfly Hill
Missoula Eulogy, Lunar Perigee, Great Falls Revelation:
  To Jake Woirhaye
Heart: *To Craig and Sophie Sheppard, Jim McCormick, and Fred Reid*
Pilgrimage—Great Falls, Montana, 1995: *To Joe De Yong*
Darkroom Fixer: *To Roger Thibault—*
  In Memory of Quinton Duval and Curt Stewart
Gumbo: *To Curt Stewart*
Arterial Hemoglobin Blood-Oath Resolution: *To Marlagayle Painter*
Double Sixes, Double Six-Guns: *To Red Shuttleworth*
Modern Medicine: *To Dr. Gregg Pike*
Science Fiction Wish: *For Cody, and In Memory of Barbaro*
Migraine Hangover—The Agonizing First Smile: *To Heather Hafleigh*

Cigar Box Chocolates: *To Doris Porch*
What Stephen Hawking, the Definitive Poet of All Time,
Might, As We Speak, Be Coming Face-To-Cosmological-Face
With: *To Clare of Assisi—The Patron Saint of Television*
Furthur-Bless-America Big-Bang Future-Flashback Boogie:
   To Ed McClanahan & Ken Kesey
Boom Or Bust, But Do Not Trust The Judges...
   To the Victims of the Iraq War
The Pedophile Priest Enters The "Wanted: Dead, *Not* Alive"
   Prayerless Lair Confessional Of His Prey:
   To the Victims of the church
Life So Far: *To Peter O'Brien*
Dying To Live Like Hemingway: *To Kim Zupan*
Two Takes On What's Left: *To Elizabeth "Buzzy" Vick*
Deep Hidden Meaning, Deep Hidden Morning on Mute:
   To Dr. Bonnie Friehling
Ink Still Wet: *To My Mother, Delia*
Living Poetry: *To Elizabeth Dear*
Grace: *In honor of Mary E. Moore*

Acknowledgments

With much gratitude to the following publications and their editors for so generously gracing my works, some in earlier rendition and/or under different title, with their first homes in print:

EMBROIDERED STORIES: Interpreting Women's Domestic Needlework from the Italian Diaspora (University Press of Mississippi, 2014)—"Ink Still Wet"

BECOMING FLIGHT: The Heavy Guide to Ornithology (Ltd. Ed. Handmade Book by Michael Koppa, The Heavy Duty Press, 2004)—"Vigil"

51: 30 POEMS, 20 LYRICS, 1 SELF-INTERVIEW (Bangtail Press, 2011)— "What Stephen Hawking, The Definitive Poet Of All Time, *Might*, As We Speak, Be Coming Face-To-Cosmological-Face With" Recorded on *COLLISIONS OF RECKLESS LOVE* (Open Path Music, 2005)

WOLF TRACKS ON THE WELCOME MAT (OreanaBooks, 2003) —"How The Beluga Spoons." Recorded on *COLLISIONS OF RECKLESS LOVE* (Open Path Music, 2005)

Montana Quarterly—"Gumbo," "Vigil," "Dying To Live Like Hemingway," "Modern Medicine," "The Wild Arrival," "Interplanetary Hernia Ultrasound." (Thanks, editor in chief and friend Scott McMillion, for your slight-of-hand inclusion of poetry into your magazine—for trusting my work to engage your prose readership.)

The Big Sky Journal—"**Click...Click...**," "Deep Hidden Meaning, Deep Hidden Morning On Mute"

The Cream City Review—"Salt Water Love"

Cedilla / 5: A Montana Trip —"Missoula Eulogy, Lunar Perigee, Great Falls Revelation"

Right-This-Fucking-Minute (Bunchgrass Press, 2012)— "Informally In Memoriam"

The Chariton Review—"Winter Solstice 10-Count," "Endorphins"

Elkhorn Review—"Loving The Mamba"

Spit in the Ocean #7—"*Furthur*-Bless-America Big-Bang Future-Flashback Boogie"

The Ohio Review—"Life So Far"

The book and section epigraphs were chosen from a file titled "Zarzyski Dictums," numbering over 500 entries at the time of this publication—personal, philosophical proclamations focusing on poetic, socio-political, primarily visceral approaches across the spectrum to living-n-dying navigations on planet earth from a single being's unique, yet humanly flawed, vantage point.

Genuflections

My most fervent shout-out to musician, music producer, photographer—all-around Renaissance man, deep into his soul's DNA helices—**Gordon Stevens**, who documented somewhere in Wyoming another PZ who, carved in bark, lives on. Gordon's front-cover image, unframed and unimpeded by text, poetically beckons viewers to venture into the aspen stand, into the "quakies," and to engage—via whatever courageous teleportation spirit they can evoke—their own *Going It Alone* journeys.

Further heartfelt gratitude to **Jessica Brandi Lifland** for her decades of capturing the most radiant light in which performers, staff, and fans basked at the National Cowboy Poetry Gathering in Elko, Nevada, where she framed—mere seconds before I, solo, forked the stage for a wild rodeo-poetry ride—the definitive "Going It Alone" back-cover photograph.

Kudos to graphic designer **Monica Sousa** for her artistically alluring front-n-back cover concepts, to **Sande De Salles** for her critically discerning eye throughout the long evolution from photograph to finished cover, and to **Allen Jones** for his burnishing of the final rendering. Appreciation also to **Elizabeth Dear** for her input.

Thank you to outside readers extraordinaire, **Gary Thompson**, **Sally Phelan**, **Andrew Guschausky**, and **Spike Barkin**, the latter who proclaimed (prior to **Allen Jones** / Bangtail Press giving the thumbs-up to the manuscript), "I can see how Section Four would frighten any publisher." **Spike**, obviously, does not know **Allen Jones**.

Finally, let it be forthrightly acknowledged that the title of this book is most misleading on one critical metaphorical front—no way could I have "gone it alone" without the Pole Star guiding light of **Glenna Branagan**, whose steadfast friendship and diligent, meticulous line-by-line editing eye, as well as her finely-tuned musical ear, and heart, saved me often from sailing off the semantic / syntactic / syllabic ars poetica course the poems had set for themselves.

Nor could I have orchestrated this collection without my sisterly confidante, **Sande De Salles**, who, like an "ars pugilistica" trainer, pushed me toward another, and another, and yet another mile of "roadwork in the boneyard" as my "Extreme Creativist" 8-banger ticker ran on fumes—especially so, regarding this book's choreography. Thank you Sande for keeping my work up on its toes and poetically dancing out onto the canvas for another round.

Title Index

About the Author

Paul Zarzyski—recipient of the 2005 Montana Governor's Arts Award for Literature and author of a dozen collections, including this third volume from Bangtail Press—has written poetry for fifty years. In the early 1970s, while studying with Richard Hugo, Madeline DeFrees, Quinton Duval and Gary Thompson in the Master of Fine Arts Creative Writing Program at the University of Montana, he chanced upon rodeo, bareback bronc riding, a passion that seeped osmotically into his work. His first full collection, *The Make-Up of Ice* (University of Georgia Press, 1984), is divided into two sections, the opener set in Montana, while the closer is set in his childhood home ground, Hurley, Wisconsin. This pull between the West and Midwest continues to this day, as he returns often to the very same home (albeit in the sad absence of his parents) to write in the very same kitchen where his mother "dribbled just a little" coffee into his baby bottle, she confessed decades later, after her infant son vigorously tugged at her cup with glee.

In light of his early affinity for caffeine sipped in the midst of his immigrant mother's symphonic Italian nursery-rhyme lilts, in the midst of his Polish iron-ore-miner/outdoorsman/WWII Veteran father's animated storytelling patina'd in visceral vernacular, Paul had little choice but to become a blue-collar poet. Moreover, his work has been welcomed into the Cowboy Poetry folk tradition, highlighted by the annual "National Gathering" in Elko, Nevada, where Paul has performed for 34 consecutive years.

As novelist James Welch wrote, "Paul Zarzyski is a man of many hats—fisherman, bronc rider, son, worker, lover. From the white heat of his rodeo arenas to the calm lakes and clear streams of all our lives, this poet captures experience the way a bear goes after salmon—with confidence and patience, with intensity and purpose...."

Today, Paul is focused most pensively, albeit every bit as evocatively, on the closing seconds of his lifetime ride aboard this spinning, orbiting bucking horse orb, a ride he hopes to finish on a gravity-less note out into what he dubs "The Musical Universe of Creativity's Infinities." Writing more and more in praise of the remaining wilds of our beloved Mother Ship and his affections for the intricacies and mysteries of Her diverse life forms, "our fellow soulful beings," Paul relinquishes all distinctions, labels, stereotypes—folk art to fine art, literati to lariati—save one: Human Being Poet of, and humbled by, "The Glorious Commotion of it All."

www.paulzarzyski.com

www.ingramcontent.com/pod-product-compliance
Lightning Source LLC
Chambersburg PA
CBHW070801100426
42742CB00012B/2210